CRAZY CRITTERS

GARY A. BATTE

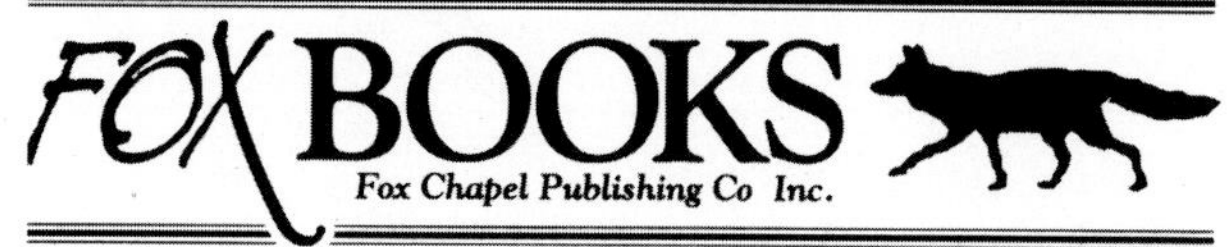

Publisher:	Alan Giagnocavo
Project Editor:	Ayleen Stellhorn
Desktop Specialist:	Linda L. Eberly, Eberly Designs Inc.
Interior Photography:	Gary A. Batte
Cover Photography:	Carl Shuman, Owl Hill Studios

ISBN # 1-56523-114-7

To order your copy of this book,
please send check or money order
for $14.95 plus $2.50 shipping to:
Fox Books
1970 Broad Street
East Petersburg, PA 17520

Manufactured in Korea

DEDICATION

This book is about caricature animals. The design and carving of these animals has been the source of much fun and enjoyment. It is to three guys who love fun and animals—my grandsons: Garrett, Holden and Dillon—that this book is dedicated.

ACKNOWLEDGMENTS

I would like to thank my wife, Sue, for her help in the preparation of this book. Besides tolerating occasional stray wood chips in the house, she provided quality control by reviewing my designs and checking my carvings for "fuzzies" and other problems. Sue helped with suggestions for projects and preparation of the text. Her support in writing this book and in all my woodcarving endeavors is greatly appreciated.

I would also like to thank my children, John and Lorri, as well as a special friend, Nell Ferguson, for their support and encouragement.

I am grateful to my many woodcarver friends who have helped and encouraged me throughout the years. I would like to acknowledge my fellow members of the Caricature Carvers of America who have inspired me to greater heights in caricature carving. The assistance of Publisher Alan Giagnocavo and the staff of Fox Chapel Publishing Co., Inc., during the preparation and publication of this book is much appreciated.

TABLE OF CONTENTS

PROJECTS

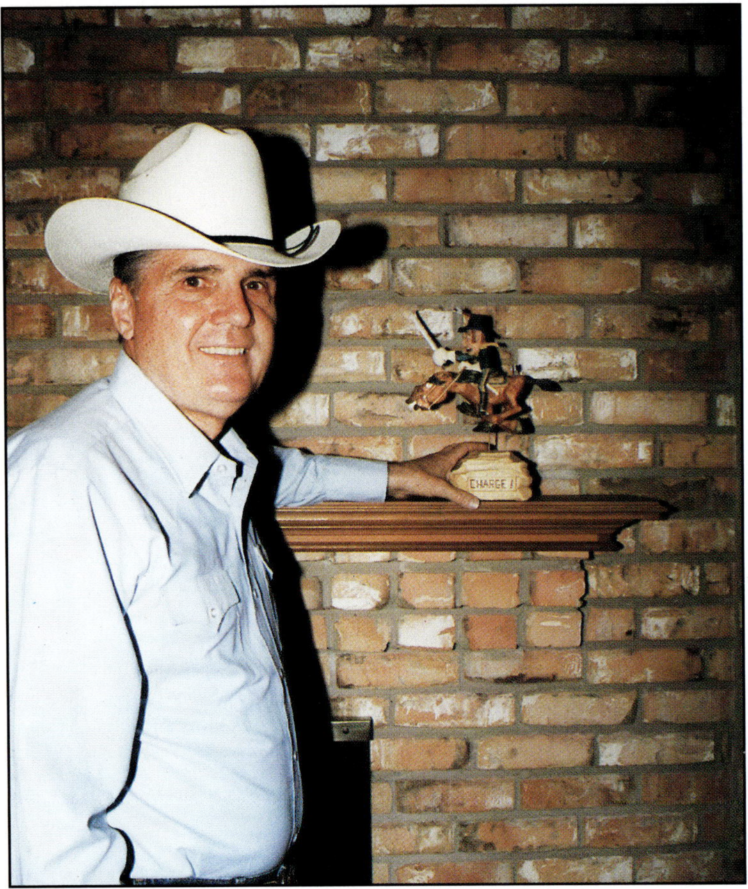

GARY A. BATTE was born and raised on a farm near Italy in central Texas. During his boyhood, Gary used a pocket knife to carve toys from apple crates and pieces of wood he found on the farm.

After high school, Gary's woodcarving talents lay dormant until he graduated from Texas A&M University and was well into his career with the USDA Soil Conservation Service. In 1979, his interest in woodcarving was re-kindled. Gary discovered that caricatures were his main interest because they were fun to carve and made people laugh.

Gary retired as Area Conservationist in 1994 and now works from his home studio in Stephenville, Texas, where he resides with his wife, Sue. He is self-taught and has won numerous awards at major shows, including first places at the International Woodcarvers Congress and Best-of-Show at the 1998 Texas Championship Woodcarving Show.

Created from original designs, his carvings are noted for their humor and detail. Cowboys and animals are his favorites. Gary's carvings have been exhibited in a number of galleries, museums and universities throughout the United States. His caricature of former President George Bush, ***Read My Lips,*** is on permanent display at the George Bush Presidential Library and Museum at Texas A&M University and appears as an illustration in the best seller ***The American Century*** by Harold Evans (Knopf, 1998). His carvings have been featured in the National Woodcarvers Association magazine ***Chip Chats*** and in ***Wood, Art of the West*** and ***Western Horseman*** magazines and other publications. Gary's carvings can be found in many private collections throughout the United States.

A woodcarving instructor for over 10 years, Gary has taught seminars in Texas and elsewhere. His first book, ***Carving Critters, Cowboys and Other Characters,*** was published in 1989. He has also co-authored two books, ***The Full Moon Saloon*** and ***Carving the CCA Circus,*** with other members of the Caricature Carvers of America.

Gary is a founding member of the Caricature Carvers of America, a select group of outstanding carvers dedicated to promoting the art of caricature carving. He is also a member of the National Woodcarvers Association, the Affiliated Woodcarvers, Ltd., and the Texas Woodcarvers Guild.

Through his persistence, Gary has developed a unique style that incorporates humor and an understanding of caricature design into his carvings.

Caricature animals are fun to carve because there are so many varieties. Each animal in this book has different carving requirements and is designed to develop and improve your carving skills. For example, Mutt McCoy (page 45) is designed and carved as a canine hillbilly complete with overalls, floppy hat and whiskey jug, while Buttercup (page 36) the cow presents exaggerated anatomical features. Caricature carving requires this exaggeration of features in order to create a humorous character. Large eyes, heads and feet are some examples. And whoever saw such a tail as that on Sweet Pea the skunk (page 4)?

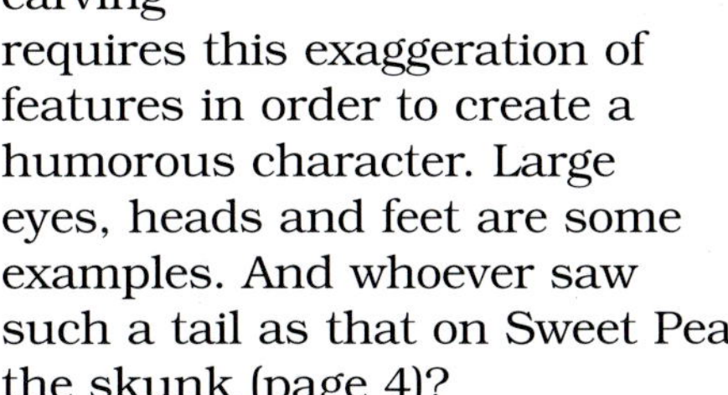

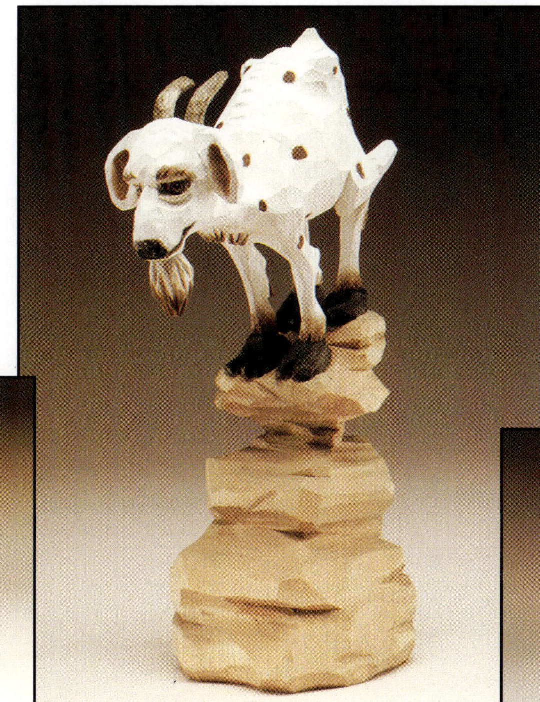

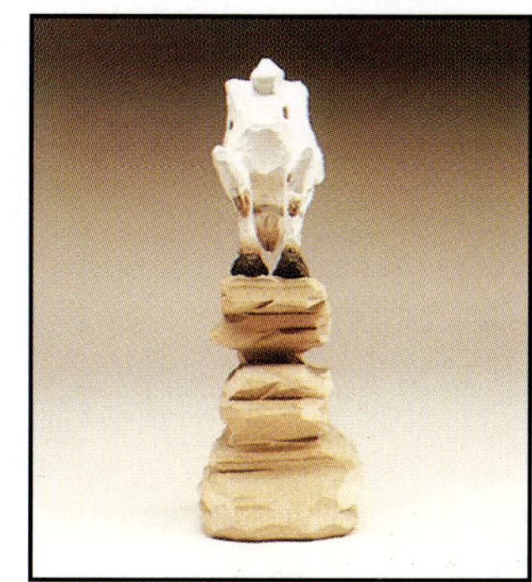

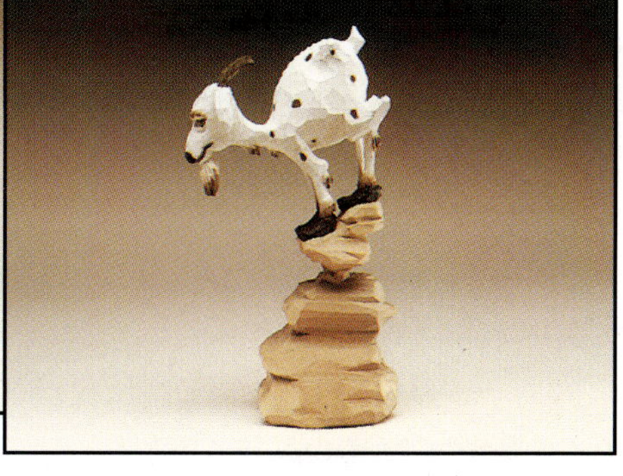

Bill E. Gote (7 1/2" tall x 2 1/2" wide by 4" deep) Created specifically for this book, this piece was sculpted from a single piece of basswood, except for the horns, which were carved separately and inserted. The grain runs vertically to minimize the chance of breakage.

The projects in this book are arranged with the easier ones first and progress to the more challenging. This book will guide you step-by-step through the carving and finishing of 10 delightful animals. Many of the common instructions, such as carving eyes, are not repeated as you progress through the projects.

All the projects start with a band-sawed basswood blank, and the carving instructions are written accordingly. The techniques shared with you in this book took me many years to learn. After carving a few of the animal characters, try designing and carving some of your own to add to your collection. This will increase the fun and satisfaction of caricature carving.

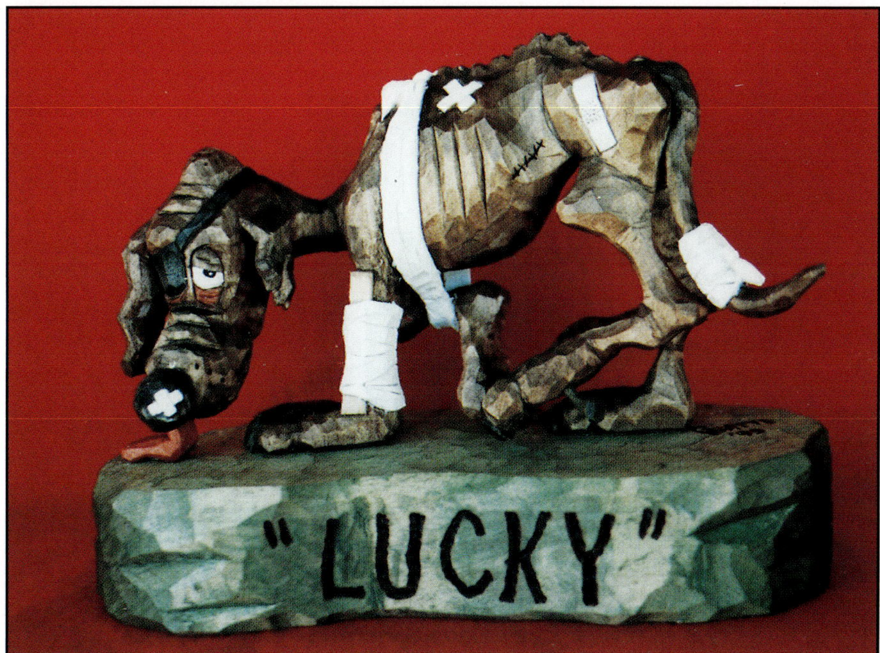

Lucky (3 3/4" tall x 5 " wide x 2 1/2" deep) Collection of John and Hazel Chaney, Wichita, Kansas. Making "Lucky" to appear not so lucky was a challenge and added fun to carving this piece. Turning Lucky's head and carving an eye patch, splints and bandages increased the difficulty of both design and carving.

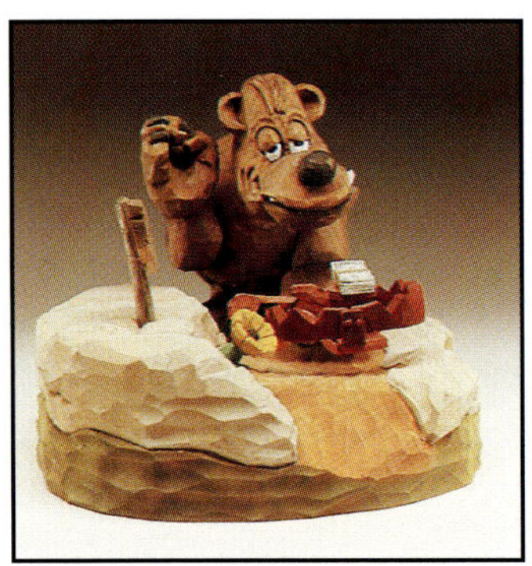

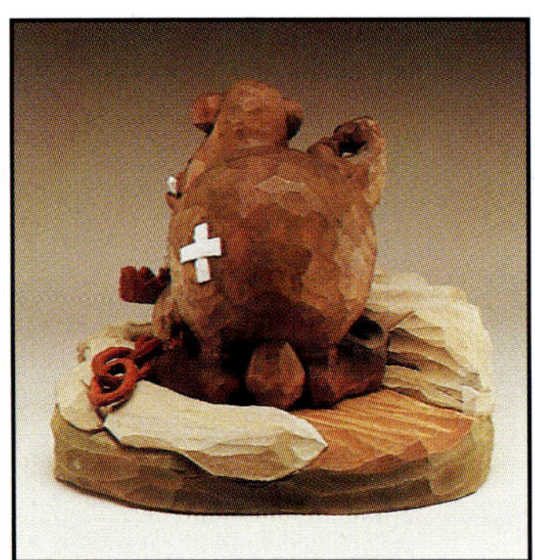

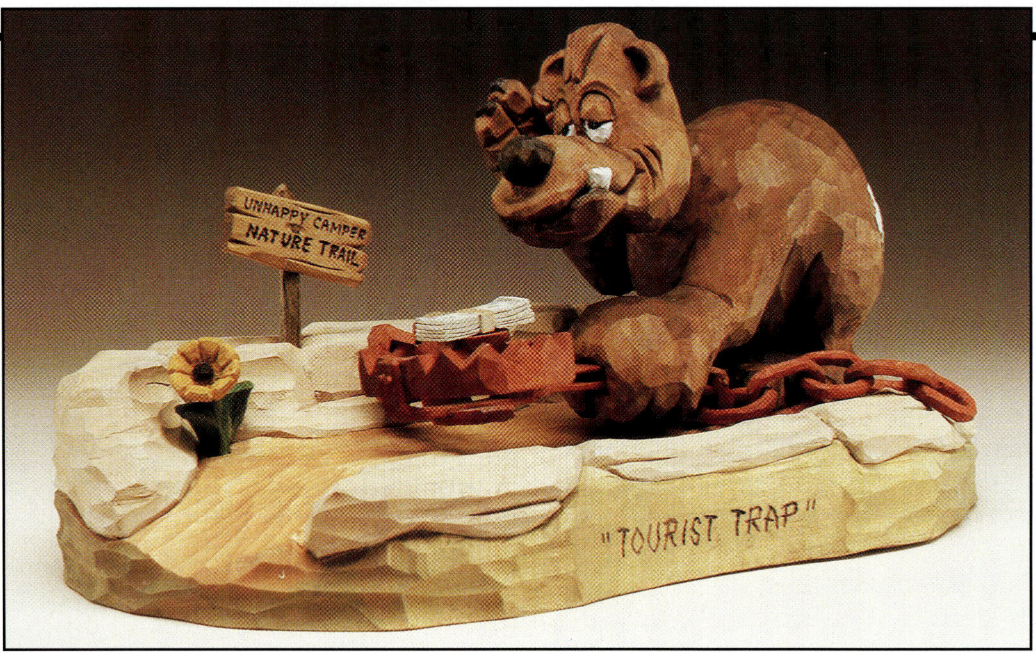

Tourist Trap (6 3/8" tall x 5" deep x 2 1/2" wide) was carved for exhibition and remains in my private collection. The base was carved separately and the other components were added. The trap was carved and assembled; then glued into place. The scene depicts a confident and smiling bear holding a large bear trap baited with a stack of bills.

TOOLS & MATERIALS

The following tools and materials were used in carving the projects in this book:

- Measuring device and pencil
- Band saw
- Carving knife
- Carving glove
- Thumb guard
- #5 – 8 mm straight gouge
- #3 – 14 mm bent fishtail gouge
- #6 – 3 mm straight gouge
- #6 – 6 mm straight gouge
- #7 – 8 mm bent gouge
- #7 – 8 mm straight gouge
- #7 – 13 mm straight gouge
- #7 – 10 mm bent gouge
- #5 – 9 mm skew chisel
- 3 mm skew chisel
- 1, 2, 3, 5 mm veiners
- 1, 2, 4 mm v-tools

Woodcarving can be dangerous. For this reason, it is important to use sharp tools. Sharp tools not only produce better work, they also require less force to cut wood and will usually do less damage if they slip. Stop carving anytime you feel fatigued, and take frequent breaks. Wear a carving glove and a thumb guard. Always cover the cutting edge of the tools when moving them from the carving area.

While this book does not contain detailed instructions on sharpening, it is highly recommended that sharpening techniques be mastered before attempting any of the projects. A tool may be adequately sharpened on stones by hand; however, this is a slow process. If tools are to be sharpened by hand, I recommend using diamond sharpeners because they are faster. After using stones and diamond sharpeners for many years, I finally switched to a power sharpener which consists of a buffer wheel, a leather wheel and two abrasive wheels. This was one of the best investments I have ever made in woodcarving equipment. I use it for all my carving tools, except for the v-tools and smaller veiners, which I still sharpen by hand. I have specially shaped pieces of leather that I use to strop the insides of those tools.

Northern basswood was used for all the projects in this book. This wood is easy to carve and finish. Good quality wood is a wise investment. Look for clear, white wood with few imperfections. Wood from the center of the tree (identified by small annual growth rings) is not recommended because it is more difficult to carve. Carving across the grain can be made easier by spraying on a mixture of 1 part alcohol and 2 parts water.

When skillfully done, painting can greatly enhance a woodcarving. On the other hand, a good carving can be ruined by a bad paint job.

I use acrylic paint exclusively on my carvings. When properly applied, acrylics give a nice stain to basswood while allowing the wood to show through. Acrylics have the advantage of drying quickly. They are readily available in craft stores in a variety of colors and can be purchased in tubes or two-ounce plastic bottles. They offer easy clean-up and are fairly easy to use.

A disadvantage of acrylics is that they tend to run and bleed over into unwanted areas. This can be minimized by first painting the area with a larger brush except for the edges; then finish the edges with a no. 00 or smaller brush. You can also use gravity to keep the paint from unwanted areas.

When it comes to brushes, try to use the best quality artist brushes that you can afford. I use both flat and round brushes of various sizes. A 000 round brush is good for small lettering.

The tip of a round toothpick can be used to paint hard-to-reach areas, such as the corner of an eye. You can sharpen the end of the toothpick, if necessary, to get into even smaller spots. A round toothpick can also be cut in two and used to paint dots. Keep the paint fairly thick and use liquid acrylics straight from the bottle when you paint dots.

A common mistake is to apply the paint too thick. Acrylics should generally be thinned with water until they are watery and allow the wood grain to show through. Mix the paint with a brush. First practice on a scrap piece of basswood. If the paint is too thin, you can always add more paint or apply additional coats. White paint usually needs to be thicker than other colors. I recommend a plastic squeeze bottle to dispense water for mixing.

Mix raw umber with the basic color to achieve a more subdued look. Paints right out of the tube or bottle are sometimes too bright. Try mixing colors to achieve new colors and shades.

I use Ceramcoat® for flesh colors. They sell three shades of flesh paint in two-ounce bottles. I use cadmium red light blended with flesh on cheeks, lips, noses, ears and knuckles. To blend the paints, apply a small amount on top of the wet flesh paint; then blend the paint with a dry brush. This same technique can be used for blending other colors.

Instead of mixing white and black to achieve gray, try using a very thin, watery black. This will produce a nice effect while leaving the wood grain showing.

Streaked gray hair can be achieved by first painting the area with white. Next dip the tip of a dry brush in fairly thick black and apply the paint in light strokes over the white while it is still wet. If you get too much black on the brush tip, remove some by brushing the tip on a paper towel.

Fine-tipped pens can be used for lettering, coloring the pupils of the eyes, and other details. I use a Pigma Micron® no. 005, which is very fine, for outlining the irises and coloring in the pupils. These pens all have black ink and are also sold in larger tip sizes. Another brand of pen that may be used is Sharpie®, which also comes in varied tip sizes and different colors.

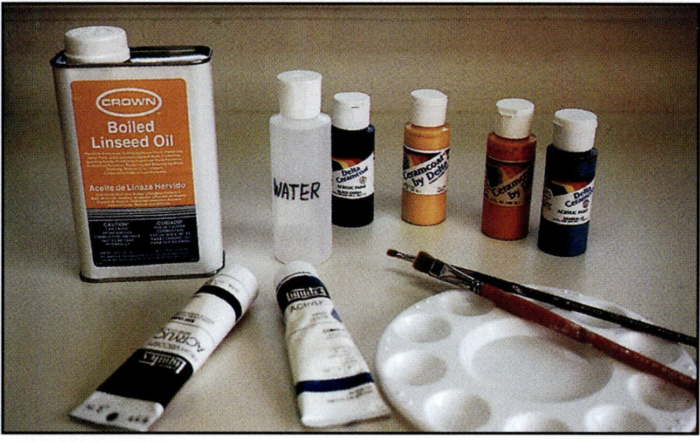

Painting and finishing materials

After the paint is dry, I seal my carvings with an antiquing mixture of raw linseed oil and raw umber or burnt umber oil paint. An antiquing liquid, usually found in craft stores, can also be used in place of the oil paint. Mix just enough of the oil paint or the antiquing liquid with the linseed oil to give it a brownish or brownish-gray color. Try it on a piece of painted scrap wood first. Too much antiquing or paint in the mixture will darken the painted surface excessively. Wipe off the excess antiquing finish with a soft cotton cloth, such as an old T-shirt, and let the piece dry.

Painting and finishing a woodcarving is an art. It requires practice, skill and patience to achieve the desired results.

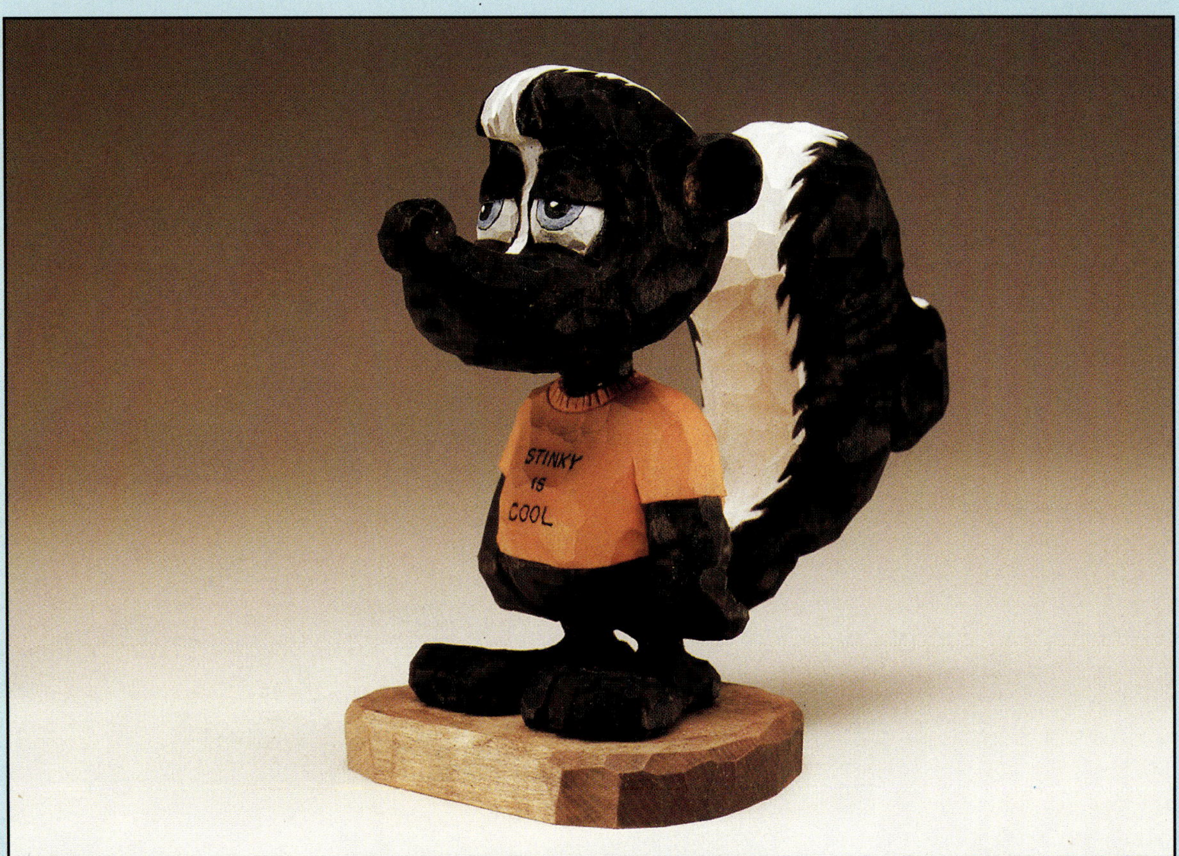

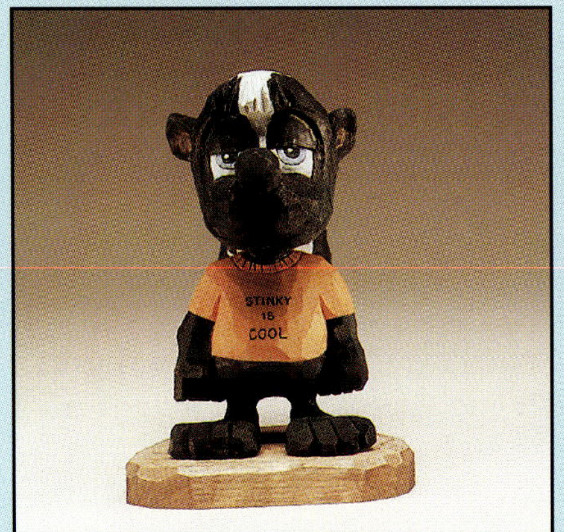

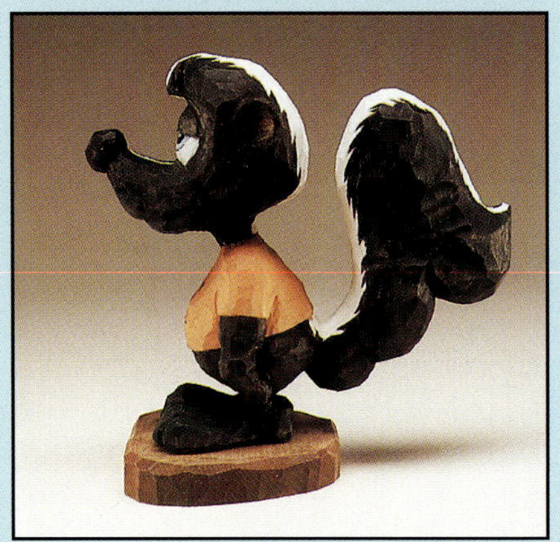

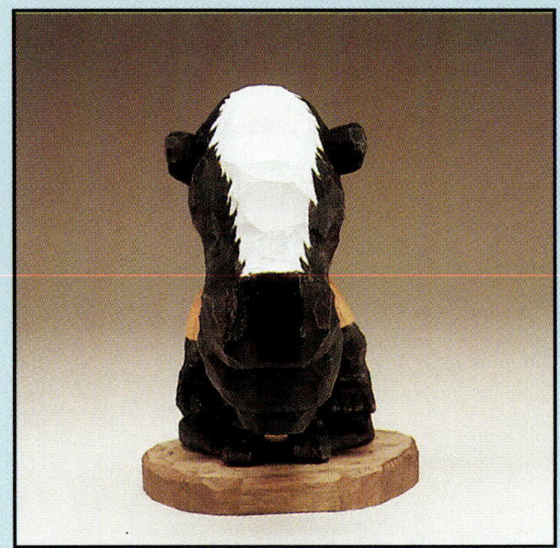

Sweet Pea is a delightful little skunk that can be enjoyed without the smell! The words emblazoned on the front of his shirt—Stinky Is Cool—indicate, however, that it doesn't bother him a bit. Along with his cartoon face, I gave Sweet Pea an oversized tail, which made him a little off-balanced. This was overcome by attaching Sweet Pea to the base.

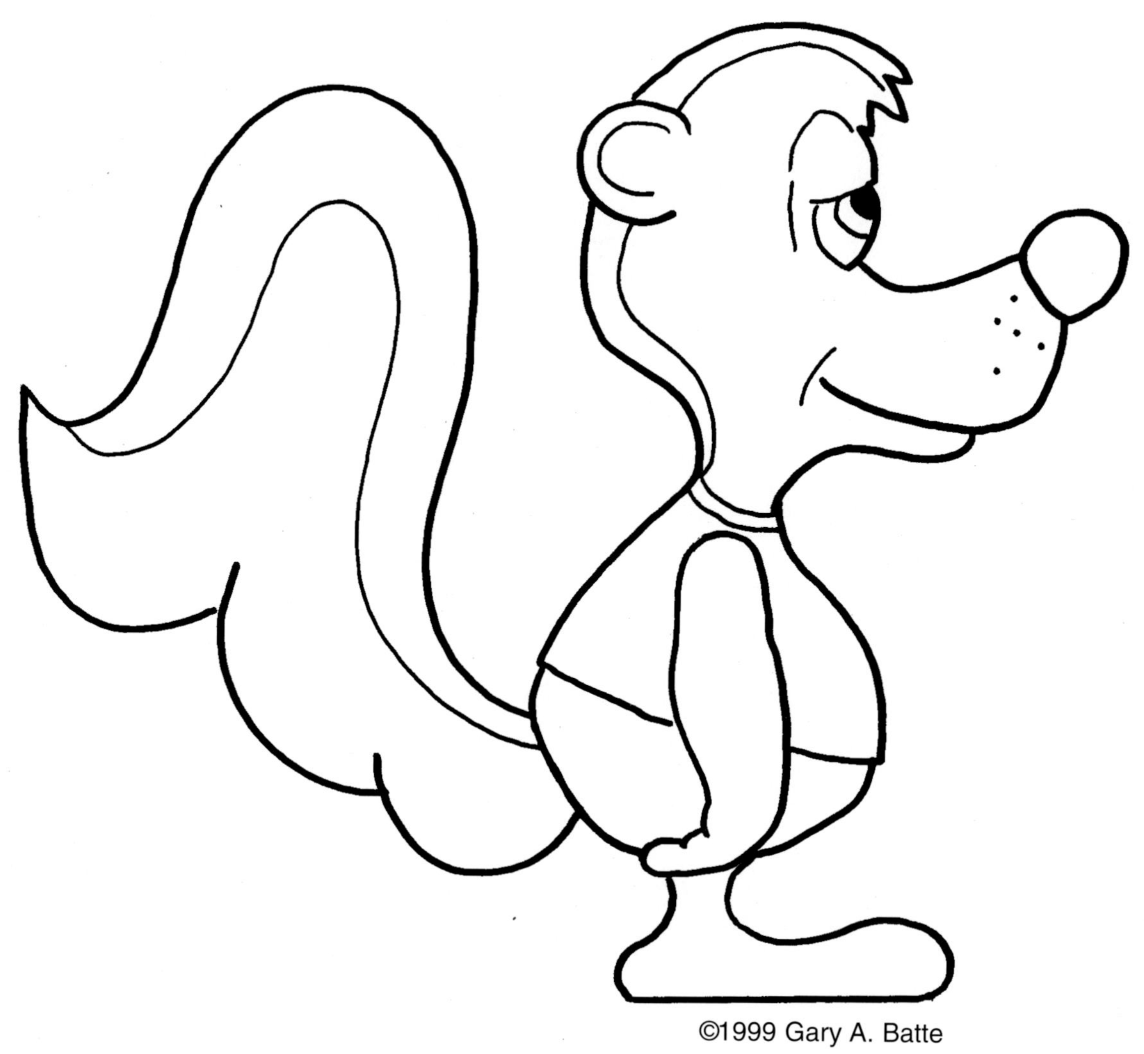

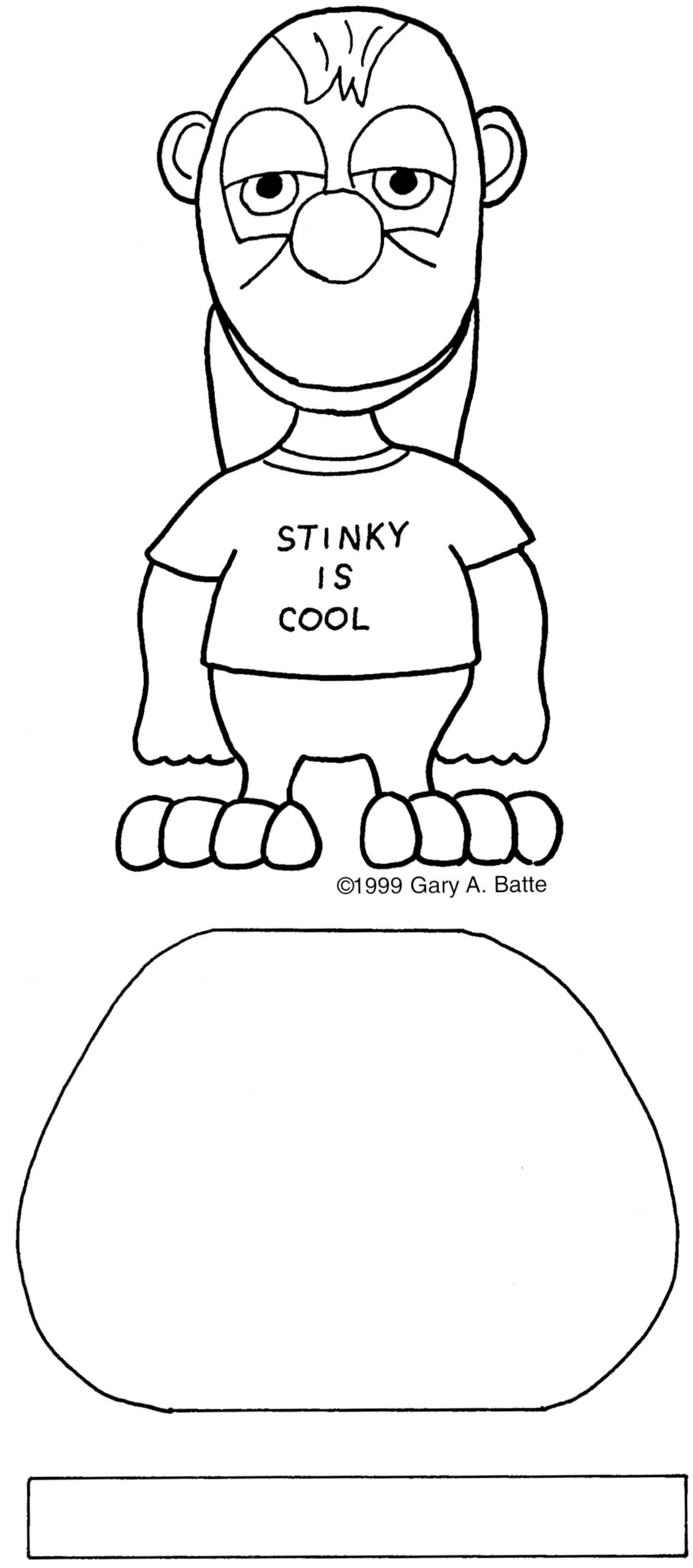
STINKY
IS
COOL

Skunks are usually cuter than they smell. This one is fun to carve, and you don't have to worry about the odor!

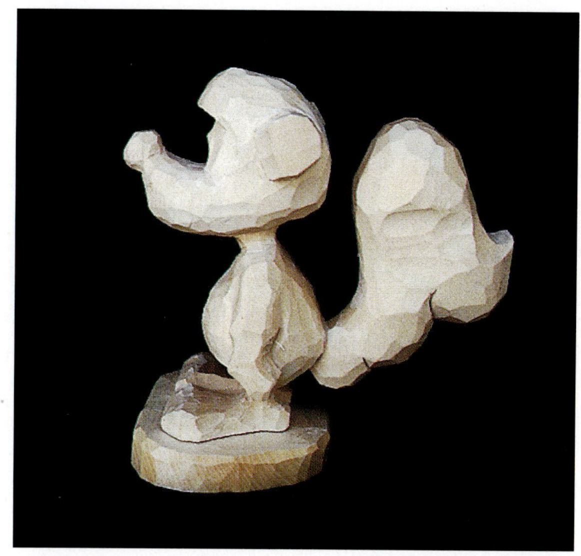
Side view, roughed out

Roughing Out

Sweet Pea is carved from a piece of wood 2 3/4 inches thick by 5 1/4 inches wide by 5 3/4 inches long, with the grain running the 5 3/4 inch length. Sweet Pea is "tail-heavy," so a base is needed to stabilize the carving. Use a piece of wood 1/2 inch thick by 3 inches wide by 4 inches long, with the grain running the 4-inch length.

Band saw Sweet Pea's side view first. Save the piece sawed from behind the legs and below the tail and tape it back in place before sawing the front view. This gives the piece stability while you are sawing the front view. Mark a centerline down the front, back and top of the piece, before reattaching the wood. Also mark a centerline down the front view of the pattern. Align this centerline with the line on the piece when marking the front view for sawing. When roughing out leave as much of the centerline showing as possible and use it as a reference point during carving.

Remove surplus wood from in front of and in back of Sweet Pea's arms, blending the upper portion of each arm into the chest and shoulder. Also, remove excess from both sides of the head to the edge of the nose. Round the head, nose and snout, leaving wood for the shock of hair in front of the head. Round and shape the tail with a knife and gouge. Shape the feet.

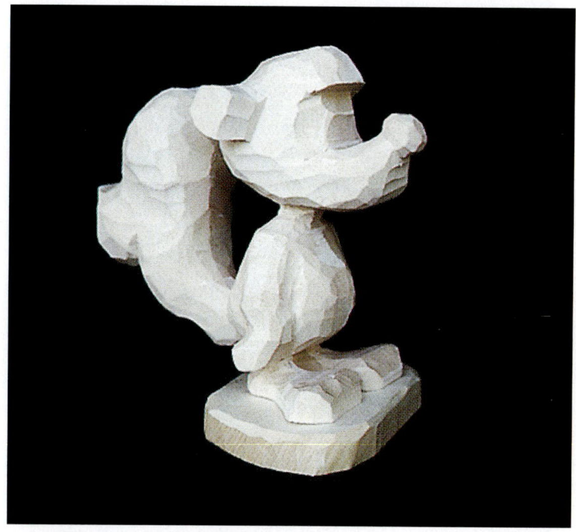
Angle view, roughed out

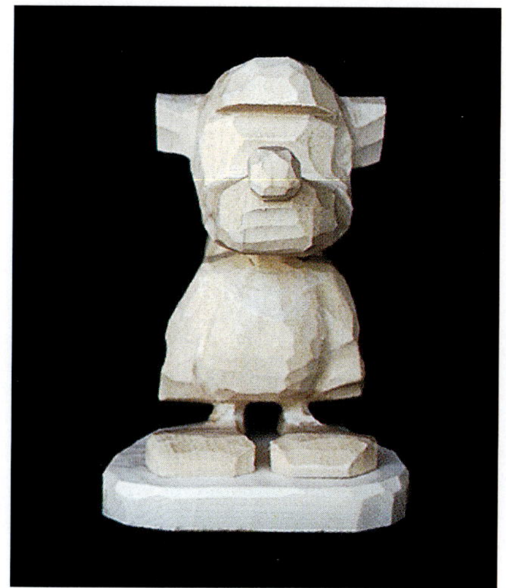
Front view, roughed out

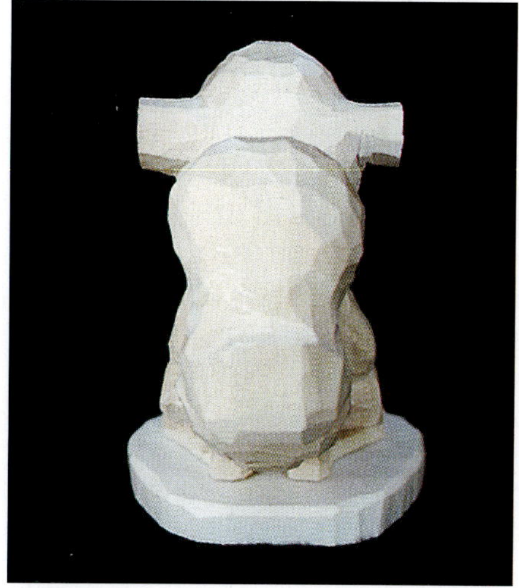
Back view, roughed out

DETAIL CARVING

Round Sweet Pea's ears with a knife and remove surplus wood from behind each ear. Hollow out the ears with a 5 mm veiner. Using the 5 mm veiner, carve around the perimeter of the large eye sockets and form the mound that forms the eyeball. After smoothing the mound, use a knife tip to make a horizontal stop cut across the center of the mound to define the eyelid. Make a similar cut around the lower half of the eyeball. Use a knife tip to remove a wedge of wood adjacent to the stop cut to define the eyelid and eyeball; then finish rounding the eyeball and the eyelid, leaving the eyeball slightly recessed. A knife and skew chisel work well for rounding.

Mark Sweet Pea's mouth line and define it with a v-tool or a knife. Round the lips and carve "smile wrinkles" with a v-tool.

Carve some hair on the forehead with a v-tool.

Round the arms, legs and toes. Make a v-tool cut where each arm meets the body and between each toe.

Carve the details of the shirt collar with a knife and a 1 mm v-tool. The sleeves and shirt tail are defined by making a stop cut with a knife tip and then removing some wood below the cut.

PAINTING AND FINISHING

With a pencil, lightly mark the separation between Sweet Pea's black and white fur. Paint the white first and erase any remaining pencil marks; then paint the black areas. Use several coats of thinned paint to achieve the desired results. The inside of the ears is raw umber mixed with a small amount of black. The eyeballs are white, the irises are cobalt blue and the pupils are black. Dip the point of a round toothpick in undiluted white paint and apply an off-centered dot to highlight each pupil. Outline each iris with a fine-tipped black pen. The shirt is pumpkin with lettering applied with the black pen. Apply linseed oil and raw umber antiquing mixture and wipe the excess off the piece immediately.

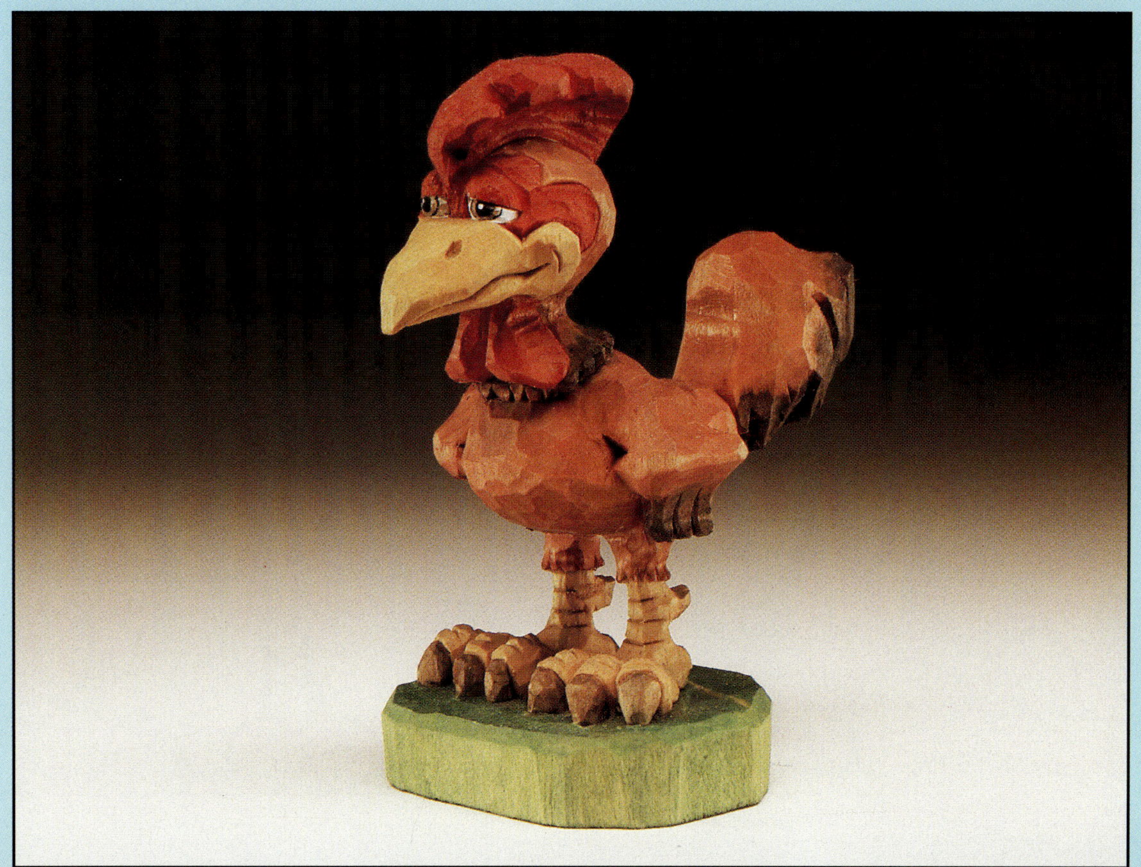

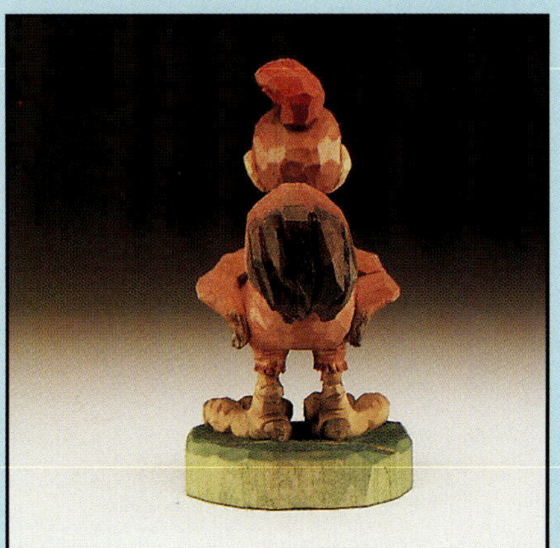

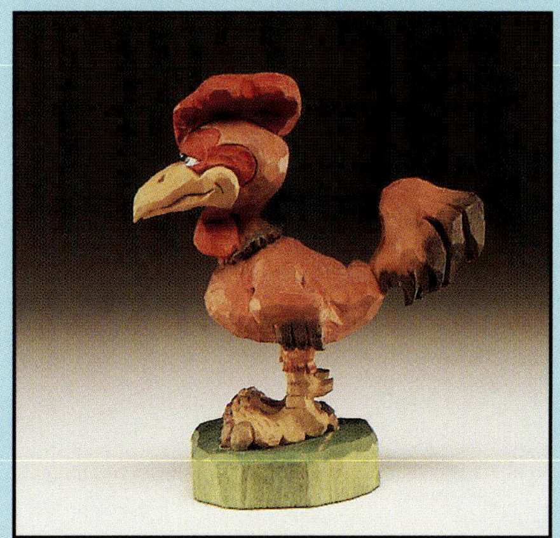

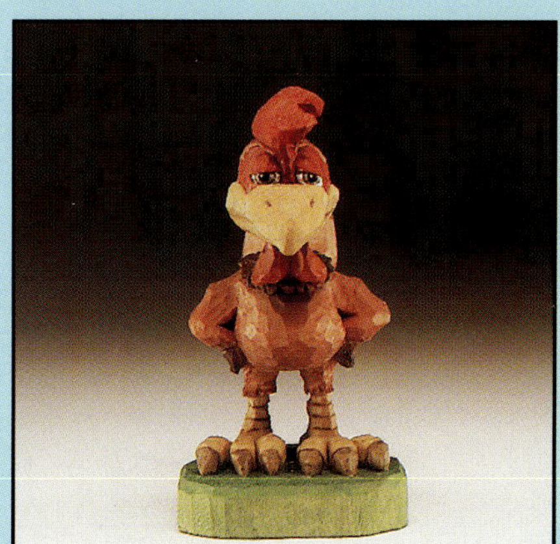

Mr. Chicken is a little rooster who thinks he is bigger than he really is. He is fairly easy to carve, with the most difficult part being the head. He can also be finished in other colors to suit the carver.

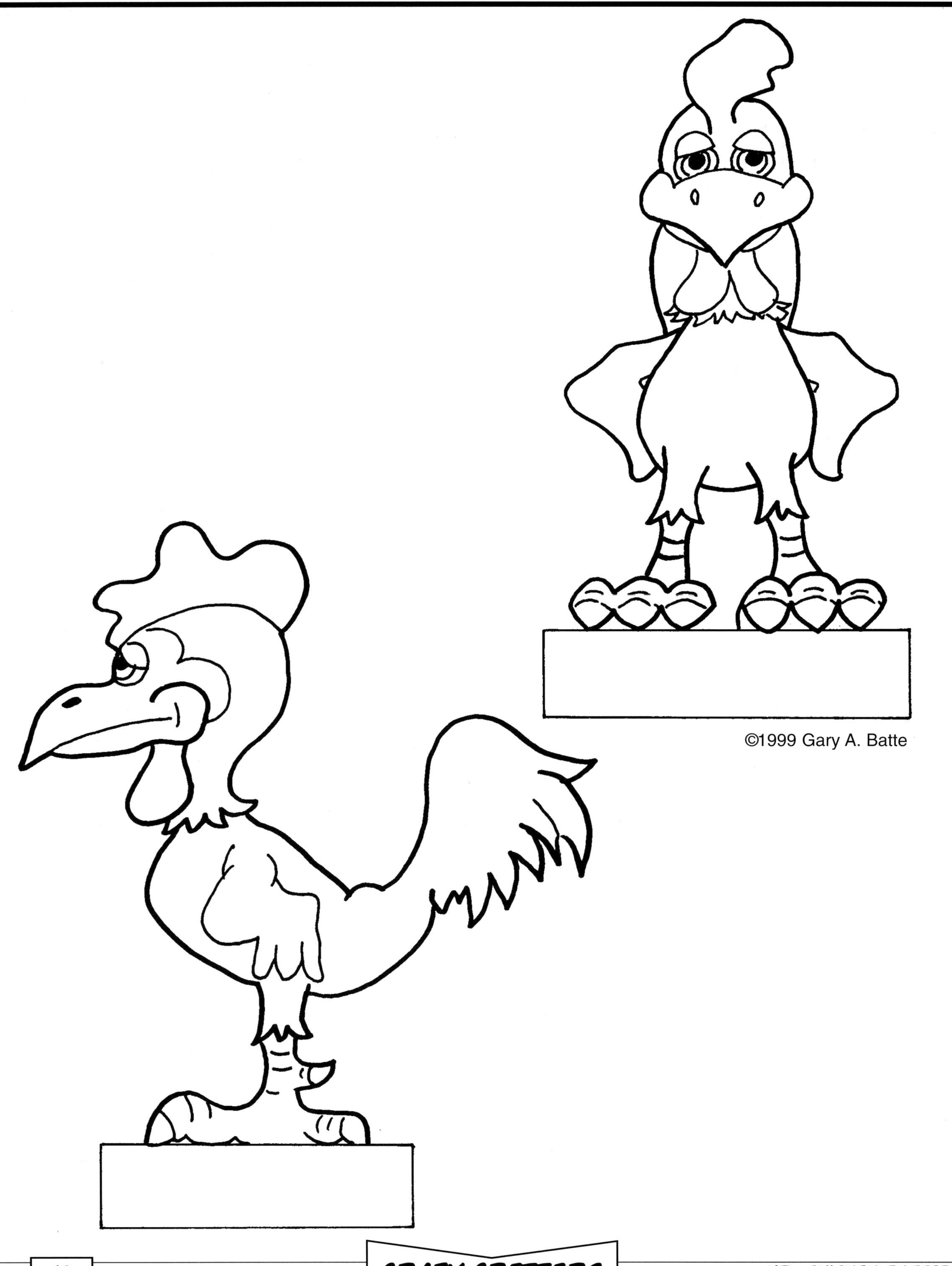

On the farm where I grew up, the old rooster was a symbol of the barnyard. He "ruled the roost" and served as the alarm clock for the other critters to wake up each morning. This little carving has Mr. Chicken posed with his wings on his "hips" as he surveys his domain.

ROUGHING OUT

Mr. Chicken is carved from a single block of wood measuring 2 7/8 inches thick by 4 5/8 inches wide by 5 5/8 inches long. The grain runs the 5 5/8-inch length. Both the rooster and the base are carved in one piece. (The toes would be easily broken if Mr. Chicken were carved separately.)

After sawing, make sure the front view of the head and neck is marked, including enough width to accommodate the wattles that hang below the chin. Remove excess wood from the sides of the neck and head.

Mark the top view of the feet and the front view of the legs. Carve excess wood from the top of the base, leaving about a 3/8-inch thickness for the toes. Drill a few holes between the legs; then remove the rest of the wood with a gouge. Leave enough wood for the spur on the back of each leg. This will be carved during the final stages to avoid breakage. Carve separations for the neck and leg feathers.

Next, shape Mr. Chicken's body. First, mark the wings. Remove surplus wood from in front of and behind the wings. Taper the body width toward the tail, leaving about a 3/4 inch width where the tail joins. When rounding and shaping the body, leave enough thickness for the ruffled neck feathers. The rooster's wings are partially extended with the long feathers extending downward alongside the body—similar to a person with his hands on hips. Mark the top view of the beak; then finish rounding the body, head, legs and beak. Shape the comb.

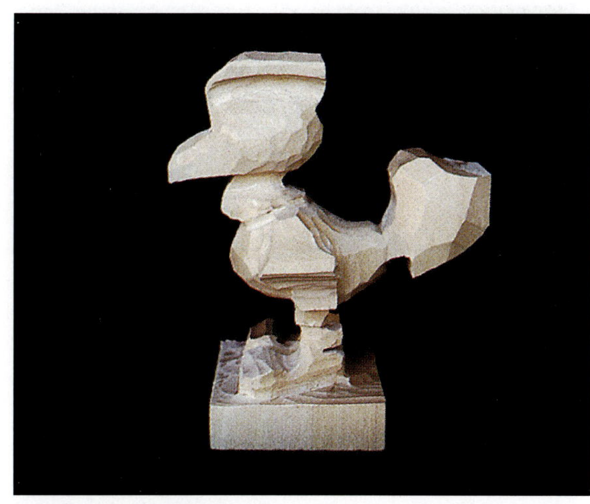

Side view, roughed out

DETAIL CARVING

Divide each foot into thirds; then mark each toe. Use a v-tool and knife to remove wood from between the toes. Shape the back toe and the spur. Use the v-tool to make ridges across the tops of the toes and around the legs. Carve the toenails and the spurs with a v-tool and a knife.

Use a knife to carve triangular-shaped separations to make the wing stand out from the body. These separations do not extend completely through the wing from front to back. Use a v-tool to carve several feathers on each wing tip.

With a v-tool, carve separations between the

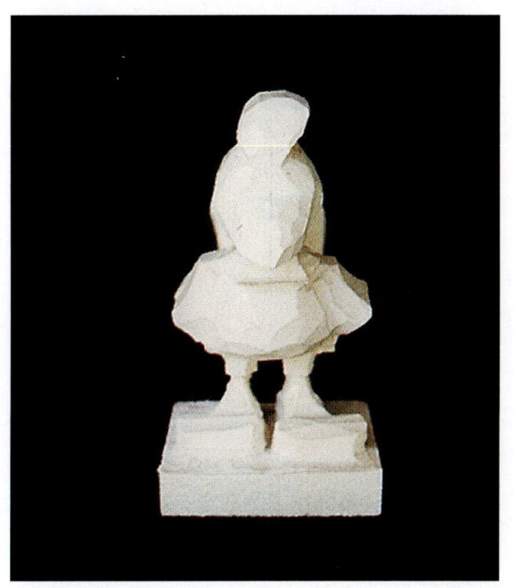

Front view, roughed out

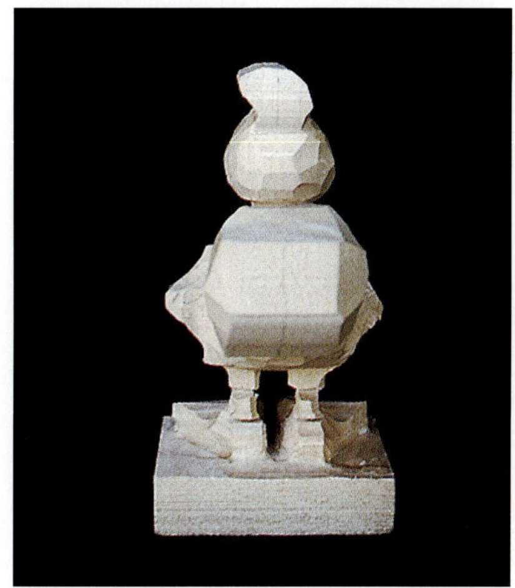

Back view, roughed out

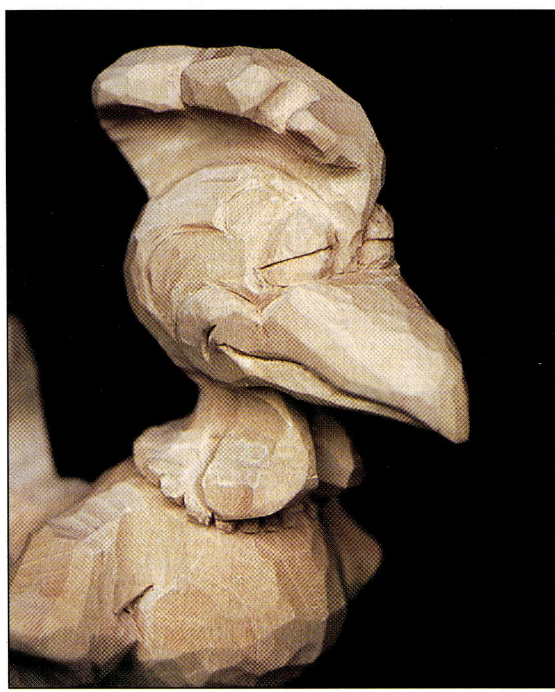

Head, carving completed

wattles and the neck feathers. Shape the wattles with a knife and a gouge.

Carve the head features. Mr. Chicken's comb bends to the left, so use a 5 mm veiner to carve inside the bend. Carve notches in the comb with a knife and a 3 mm veiner. Carve around the eye and the eyelid with a 3 mm and a 2 mm veiner and round the lid and eyeball as described in the previous project.

Carve around the back portion of the bill with a 3 mm veiner and remove more wood from the side of the head. This makes the bill stand out. Define the bill separation with a v-tool or a knife. Shape the tail and carve the tail feathers with a knife and a 4 mm v-tool.

PAINTING AND FINISHING

Mr. Chicken's body is burnt sienna with black blended on the neck, tail and wing feathers. The comb, wattles and face are napthol red light mixed with raw umber. The beak and feet are yellow oxide, with raw umber used for the nostrils, toenails and spurs. The eyeballs are white, the irises are painted burnt umber, and the pupils are painted black with white highlight dots. The irises are outlined with a fine black pen. The base is jubilee green and raw umber. Let the piece dry and apply the antiquing.

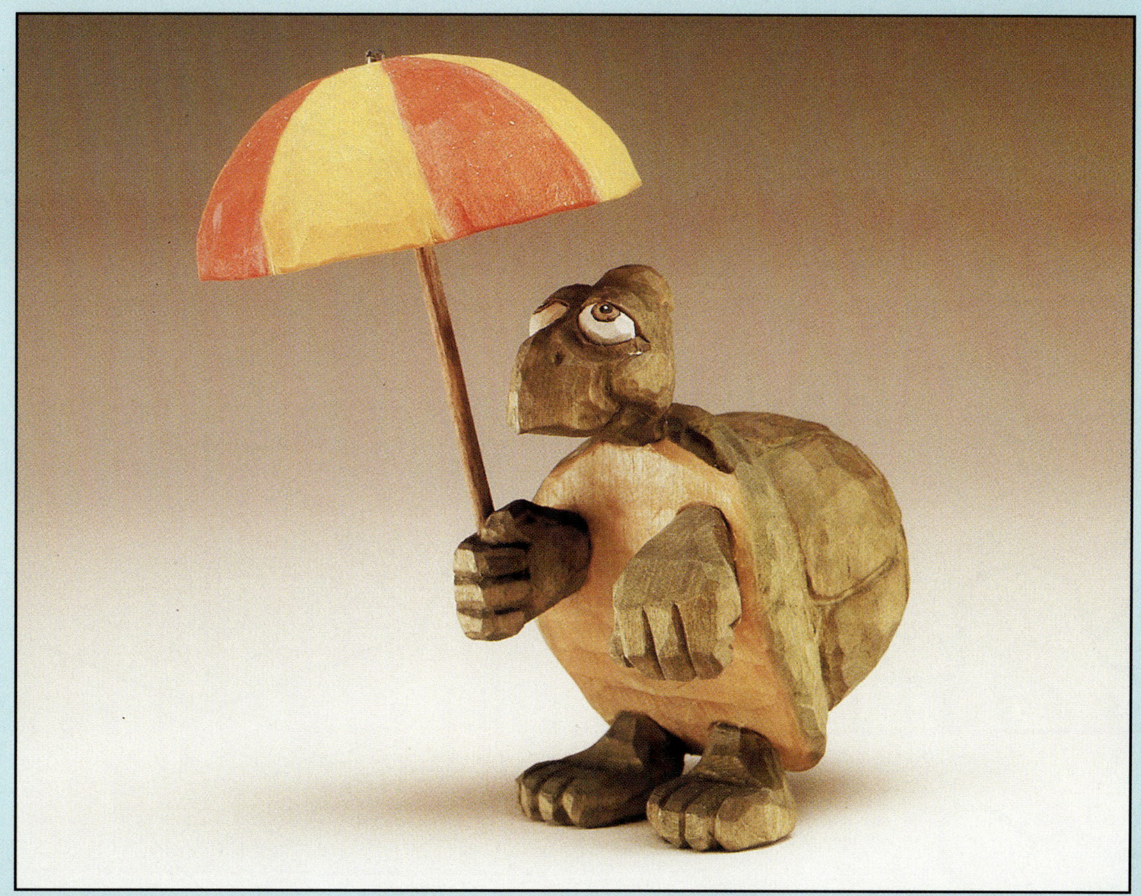

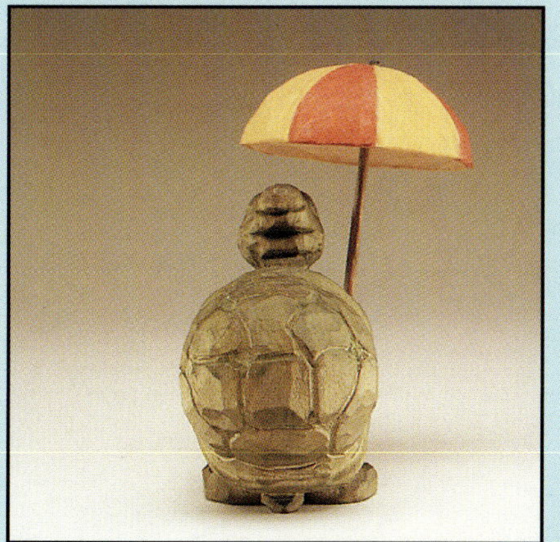

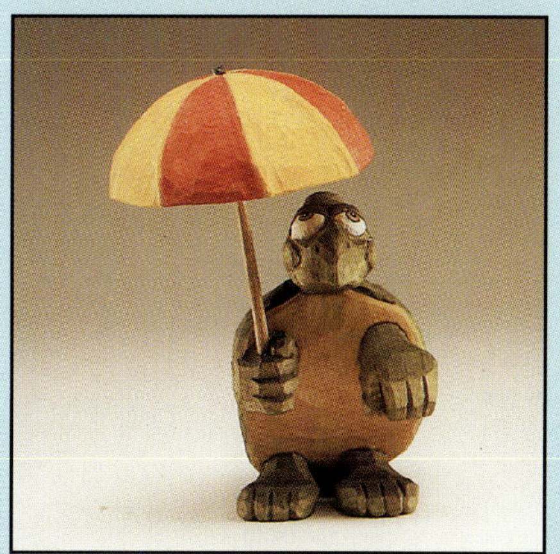

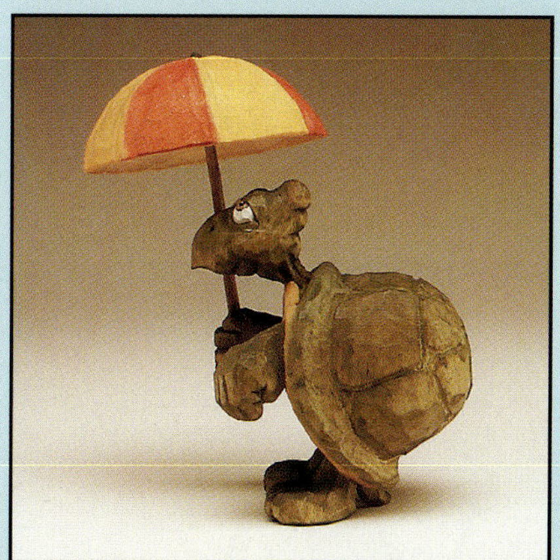

Speedy is a smart tortoise who doesn't want to be caught in the rain. He was carved from one piece of wood, except for the umbrella. Carving the "hands" was the most difficult part. Use your own hands as models.

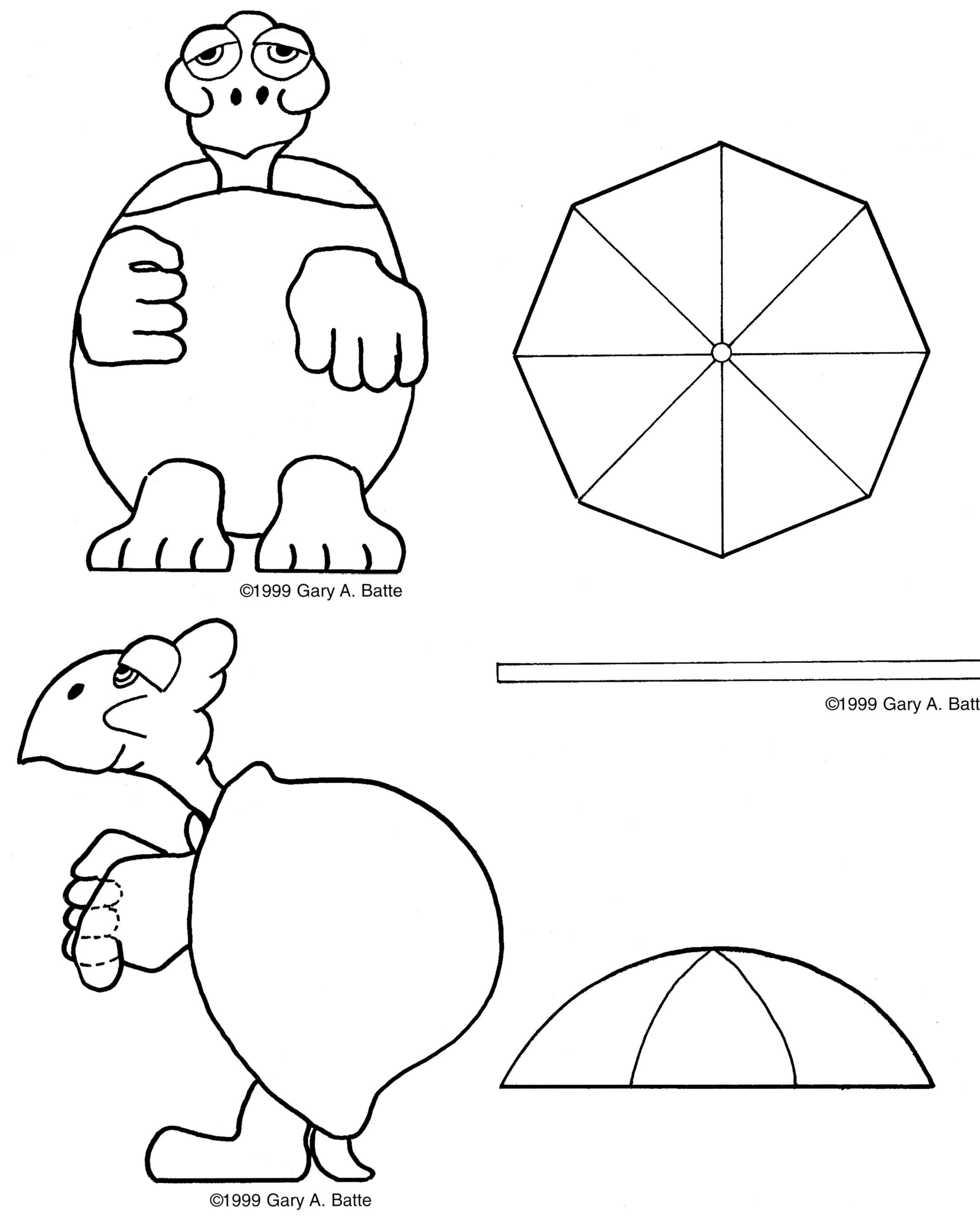
©1999 Gary A. Batte
©1999 Gary A. Batte
©1999 Gary A. Batte

Tortoises live on land where it is usually dry. But, sometimes, it does rain. Speedy is a smart tortoise and carries an umbrella for those rare occasions when it does. The umbrella was carved separately.

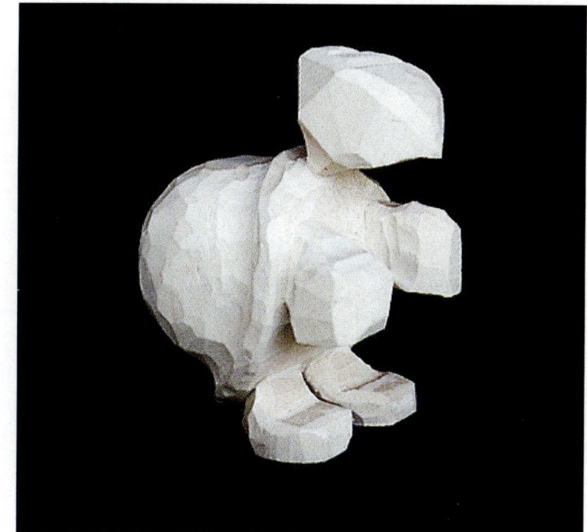

Angle view, roughed out

ROUGHING OUT

To carve Speedy, a block of basswood 2 3/4 inches thick by 3 7/8 inches wide by 4 3/8 inches long is needed. The grain runs the 4 3/8-inch length. After bandsawing, round the shell, leaving wood for the tail. After rounding, use a #7 – 8 mm gouge to carve a flair just above the edge of the shell. Round the edge of the shell.

Round Speedy's head and neck and carve the beak into a point. Leave his neck a little thick for now. Remove wood from between his legs and feet and shape.

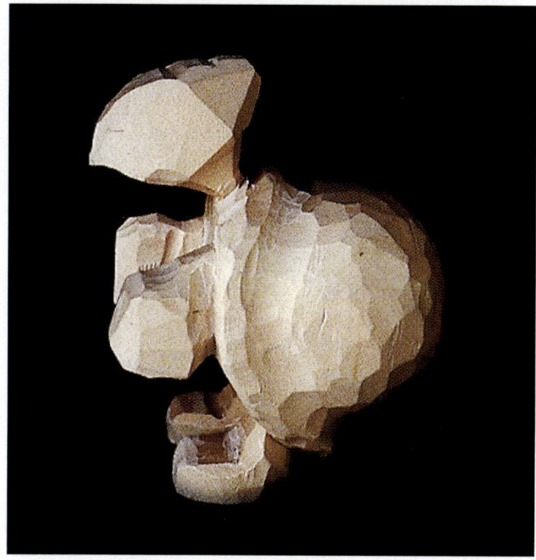

Side view, roughed out

DETAIL CARVING

Carve the foot that Speedy uses to hold the umbrella. After carving the outside dimensions, mark and drill a 5/32-inch hole for the umbrella handle. Then finish carving the toes that grip the handle. Round the toes and carve the toe separations. Carve the other feet.

Carve a groove between Speedy's eyes with a 2 mm veiner; then remove the surplus wood from around the cheeks, eyes and nose, creating mounds for the eyes and cheeks. Refer to the previous project and finish carving the eyes. Round the cheeks, continue to round the head and shape the nose and mouth. Carve the nostrils with a small veiner. Shape the neck and make horizontal wrinkle cuts across the back of the head with a v-tool. Round the edges of these cuts with a skew chisel.

Use veiners and a knife to carve an opening in the shell on each side of the neck. Shape the neck to its final thickness. Shape the tail, but leave it flat underneath to provide support.

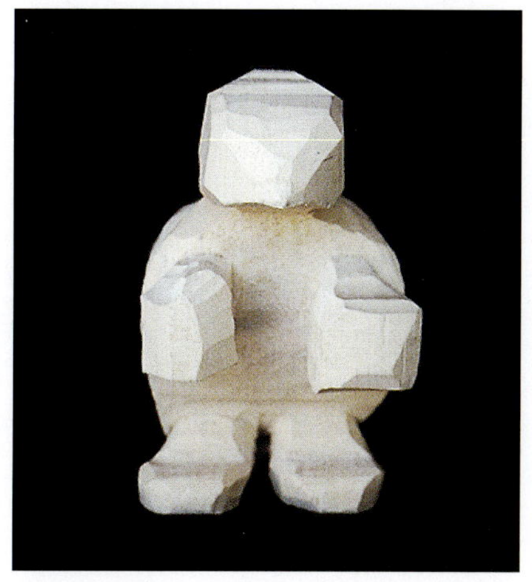

Front view, roughed out

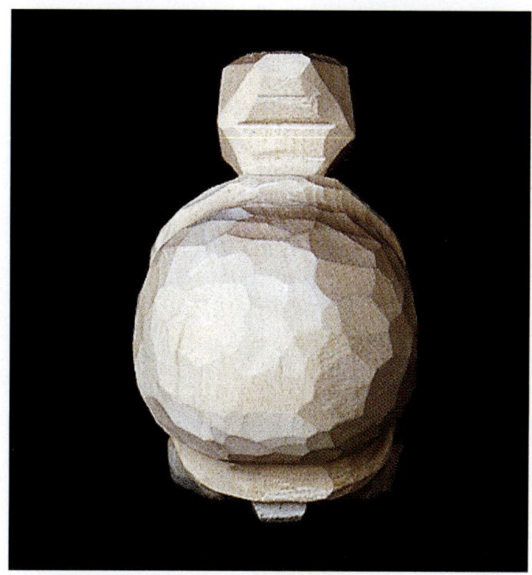

Back view, roughed out

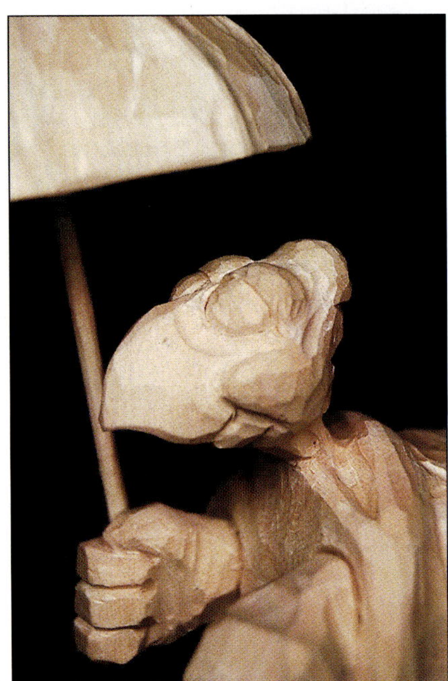

Close-up of Speedy's head and right arm, carving complete

Mark the design on the shell and carve around each section with a 2 mm veiner.

CARVING THE UMBRELLA

With the grain running with the thickness, band saw a piece of wood 3 1/4 inches in diameter and 1 1/8 inches thick. Round the top side with a knife and hollow out the inside with #7 –10 mm bent and #7 – 8 mm straight gouges. Leave the "fabric" 1/4 thick. Mark the outside of the umbrella into eight equal sections. Each division forms a rib. Remove wood from between each rib causing the ribs to be slightly raised. Now, remove additional wood from inside the umbrella as needed, being careful not to make the umbrella too thin. Drill a 5/32 inch hole in the center. Refer to the pattern and finish carving the edges. Carve the stick handle.

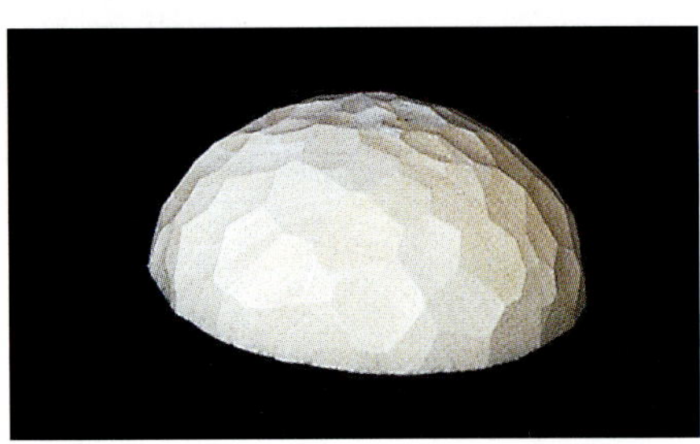

Umbrella, roughed out

PAINTING AND FINISHING

Paint the top and edges of the shell with a mixture of gamal green and raw umber. Add a little bit more raw umber to the mix to paint the legs, feet, tail and head. The underside of the shell is a mixture of yellow oxide and white. The eyeballs are white with raw umber irises, black pupils and a white highlight dot. Outline the irises with black pen. Paint the inside of the nostrils with raw umber. The umbrella is yellow and cadmium red light. The stick handle is raw umber.

Apply the antiquing. When the piece is thoroughly dry, assemble the umbrella and glue the umbrella handle into the hole in the right front foot.

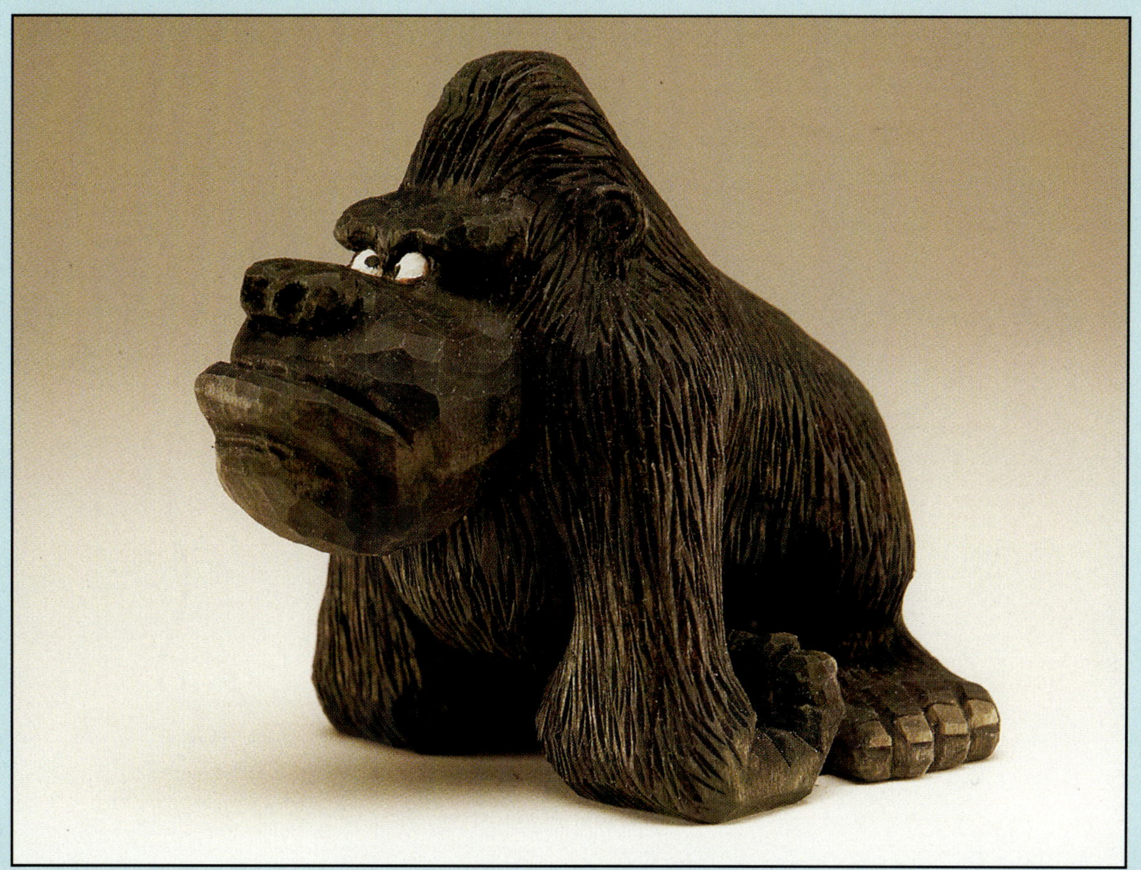

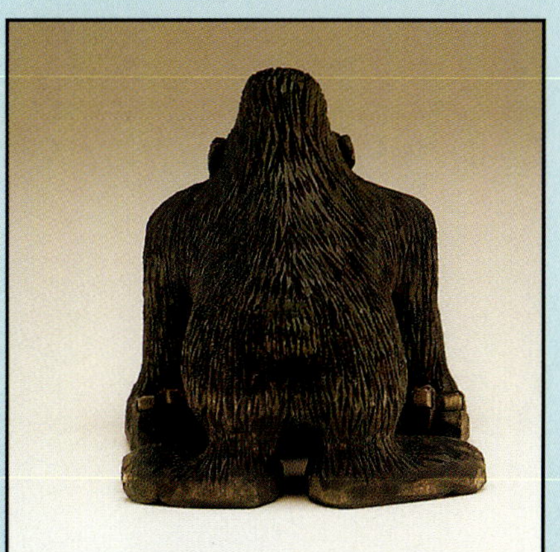

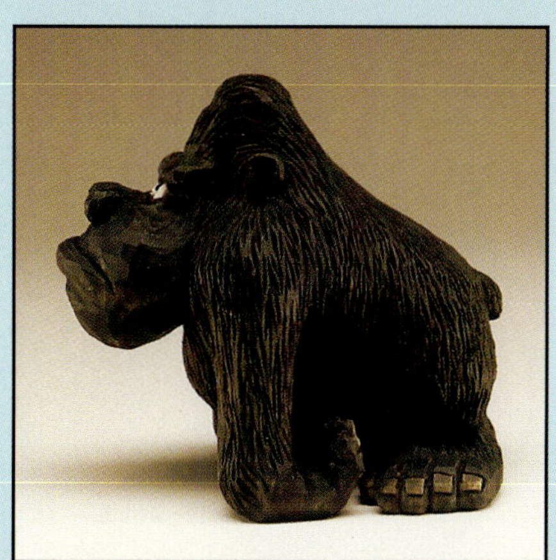

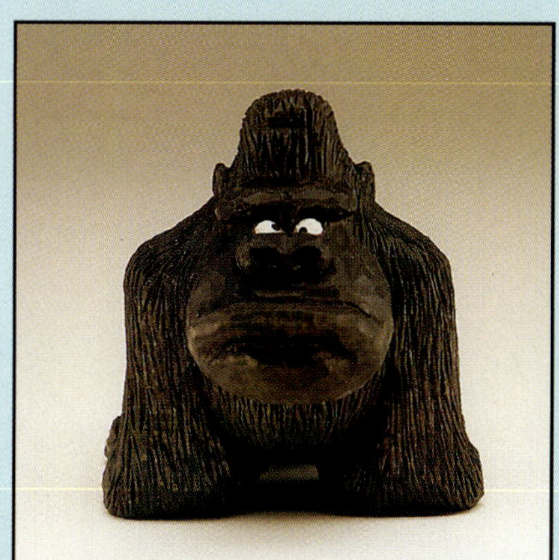

I designed Grumpy with emphasis on his physique, which was necessary to produce a good caricature. The greatest challenge in carving Grumpy was his facial expression, which is not unlike that of a grouchy, grumpy human. You can look in the mirror to practice the image you want to achieve in the carving.

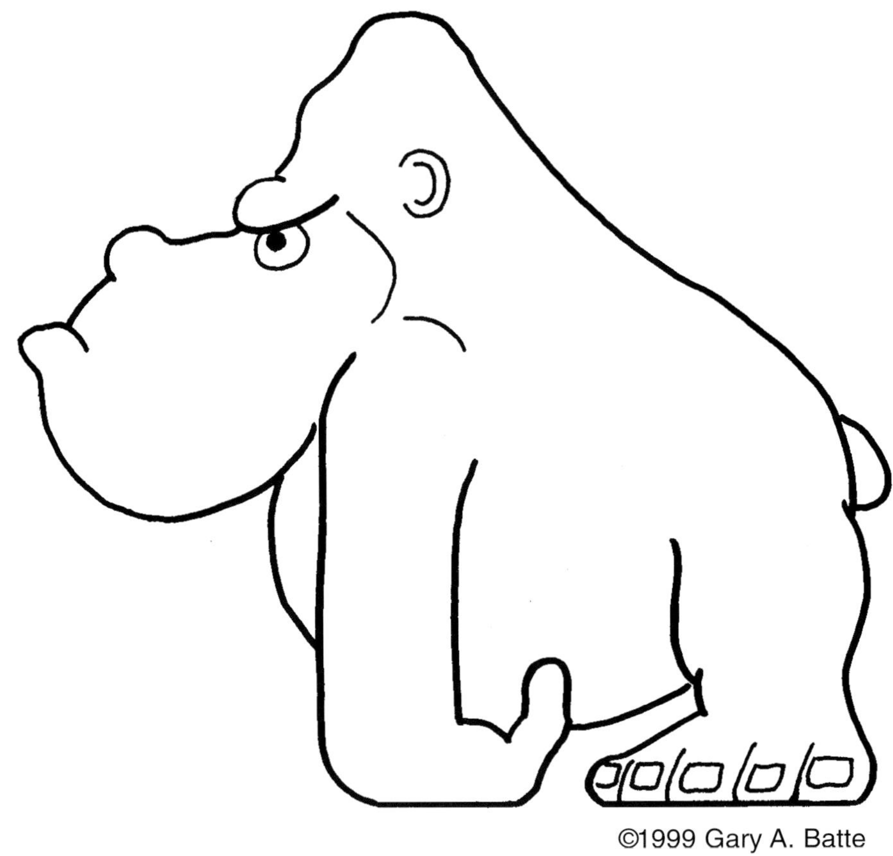

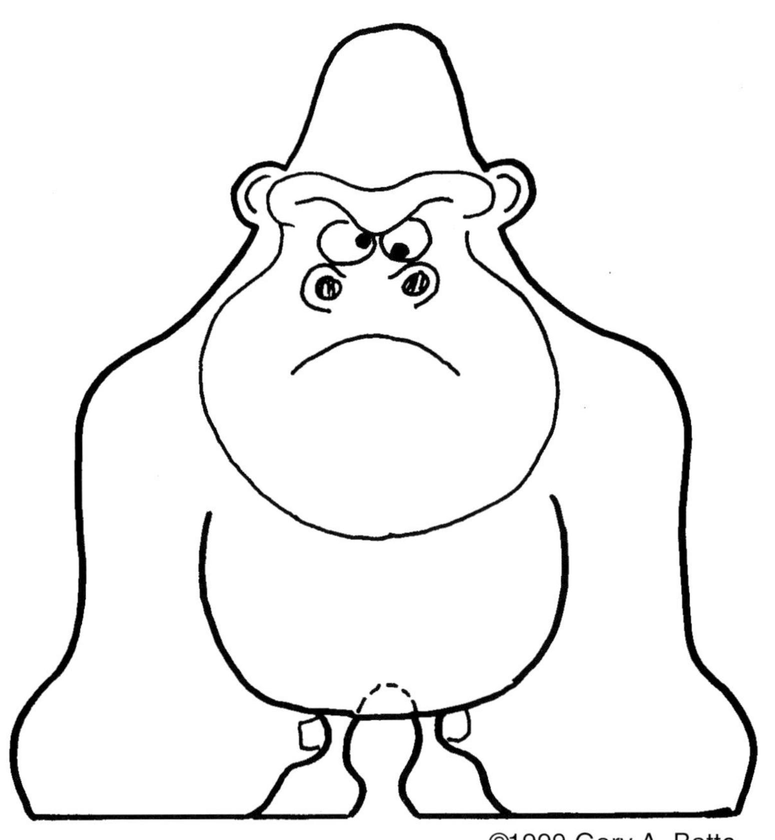

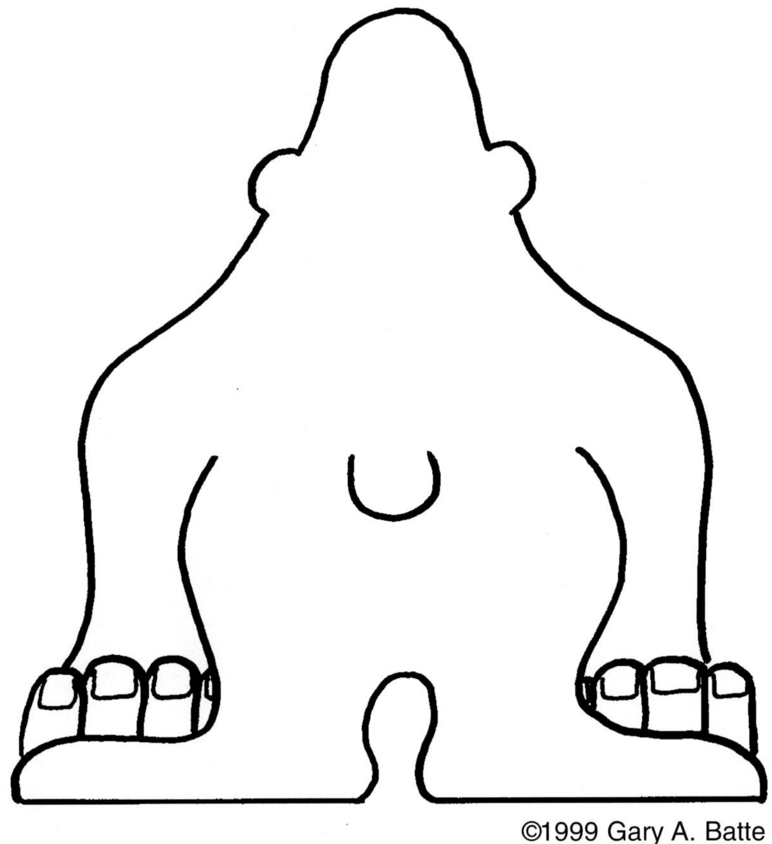

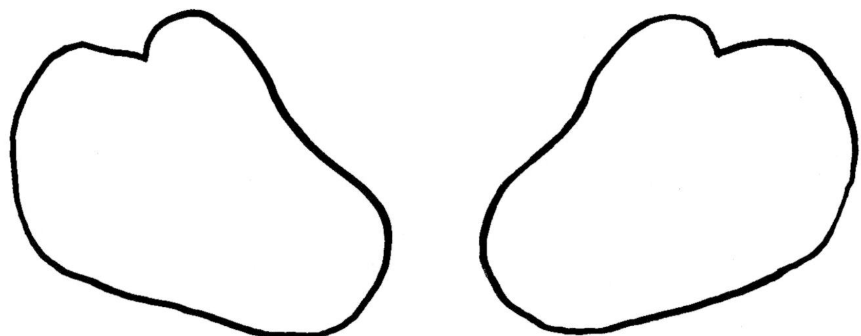

Gorillas make good caricature carvings because of their physique. They have long arms, big shoulders and short, bowed legs. They have massive bodies, small skulls, and big jaws. Although they look fierce, gorillas are shy, friendly animals, each having its own personality.

This gorilla's facial expression earned him the name Grumpy. His low, muscular eyebrow dips between two small eyes which are set close together. The lower lip protrudes and is turned down to help portray the grumpy look. Grumpy is well fed, judging from his big, rounded belly.

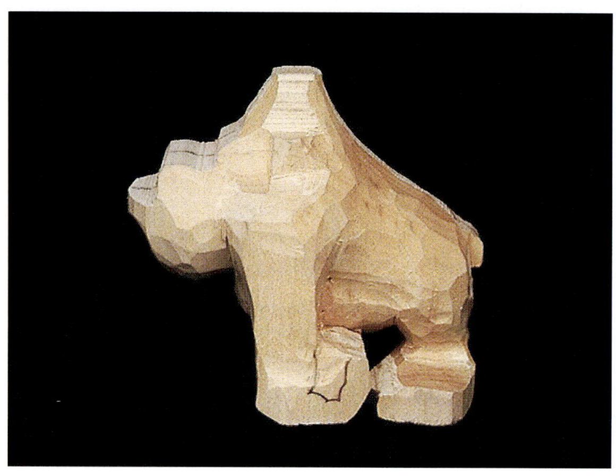

Side view, roughed out

ROUGHING OUT

Begin with a piece of basswood 3 7/8 inches thick by 4 1/8 inches wide by 4 1/2 inches long, with the grain running the 4 1/2 inch length. After bandsawing the front and side views, remove surplus wood from each side of Grumpy's head and jaws, leaving wood for the small ears. Round the head. Remove surplus wood from in front of the arms, stopping at the belly. Also remove excess wood from behind both arms and along the sides of the body. Leave a 1-inch width for the curled fingers. Round the back from the rump to the shoulder area.

Using the pattern, draw the bottoms of the feet and hands. Remove wood from between the legs. Shape the feet and round the belly. Remove wood from between the hands and shape the hands. Round the front part of the belly. The little finger of each hand will tie into the belly to stabilize the hand, so be sure to leave enough wood on the belly in this area. Round the jaws and lip.

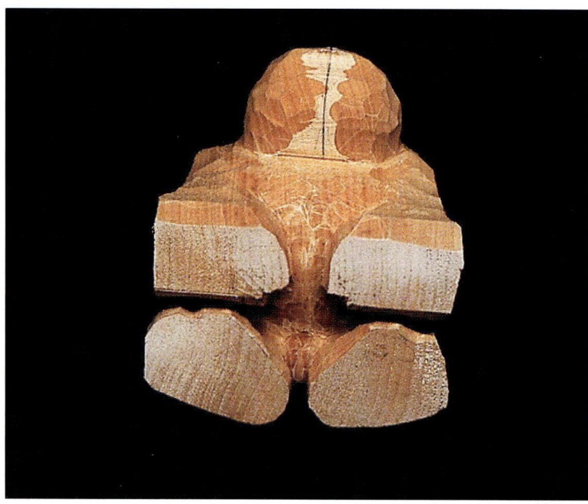

Bottom view, roughed out

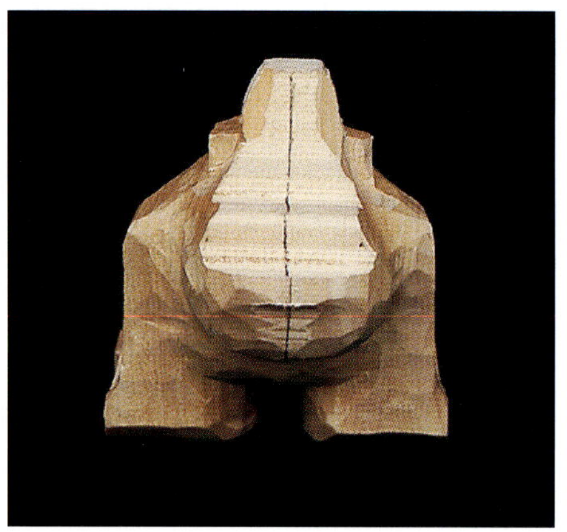

Front view, roughed out

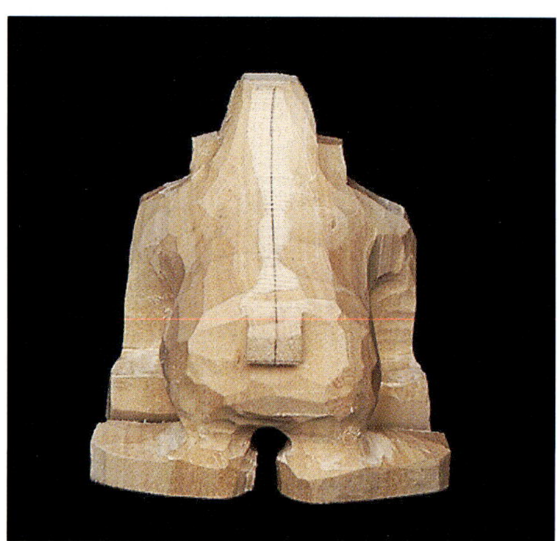

Back view, roughed out

DETAIL CARVING

Remove wood from each side of Grumpy's nose and round the large nostrils, leaving the front rather flat. Carve the inside of the nostrils with a small veiner. Mark the width of the head at the eye level and locate the ridge above the eyes. This ridge will dip between the eyes. Now, remove excess from each side of the head, leaving the skull about 1 inch wide. Round the head and the jaws a bit more so they blend in with the narrow skull and shoulders. Remove some wood above and below the brow ridge. Carve the eyes as instructed in the Sweet Pea project. Shape the lip. The bend under the lip can be made with a 7 mm veiner.

Round the ears and remove wood from the inside with a small gouge and 3 mm veiner. Use the veiner to carve a groove around the inside edge.

Round the arms, legs and rump. Shape the stubby tail.

Carve the hands. First, mark the finger and thumb separations. The little finger ties into the belly, and the thumb lies flat against the underside of the belly. With a 7 mm veiner, remove wood from the underside of the thumb. Carve the inside of the hand with the 7 mm veiner. Carve finger separations with a v-tool. A knife may have to be used for the inside separations because it is difficult to do with a v-tool. Round the ends of the fingers and the thumb. Carve the fingernails with a v-tool or a knife tip. Carve the wrinkles on the insides of the fingers.

Carve the feet and the toes in a similar manner. The "thumb" on each foot will be much shorter than the other toes.

Carve the fur with a 2 mm v-tool, making 1/4–1/2 inch cuts that are varied in angle, length and depth.

PAINTING AND FINISHING

Grumpy is entirely black, except for his eyes. Use a thinner black for the toenails. The eyeballs are white. Paint the colored part of the eyes black. The lower insides of the eyelids are crimson red light. Apply the antiquing.

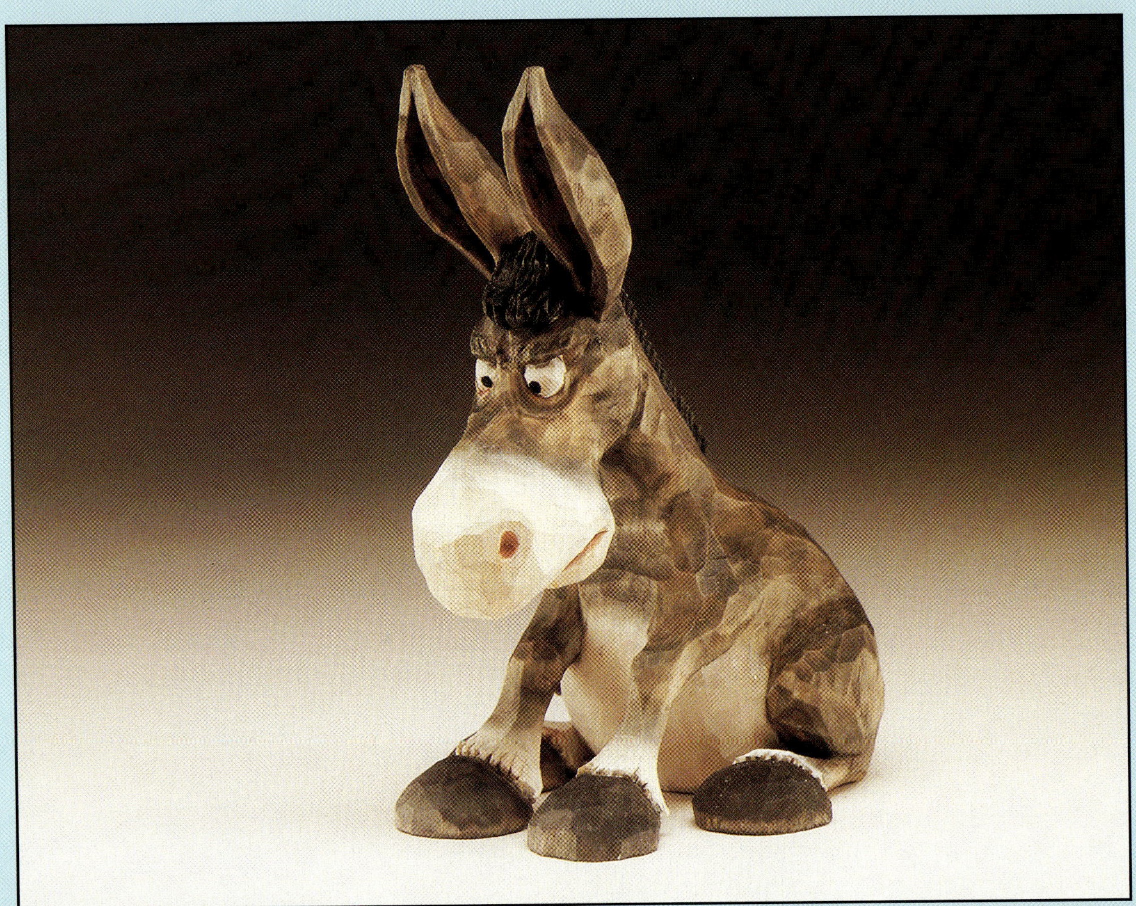

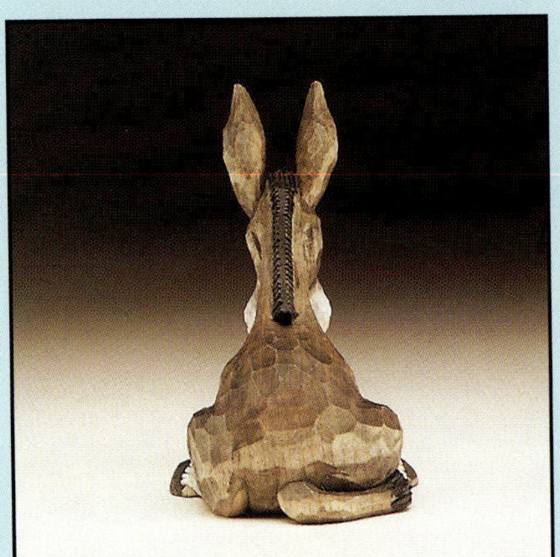

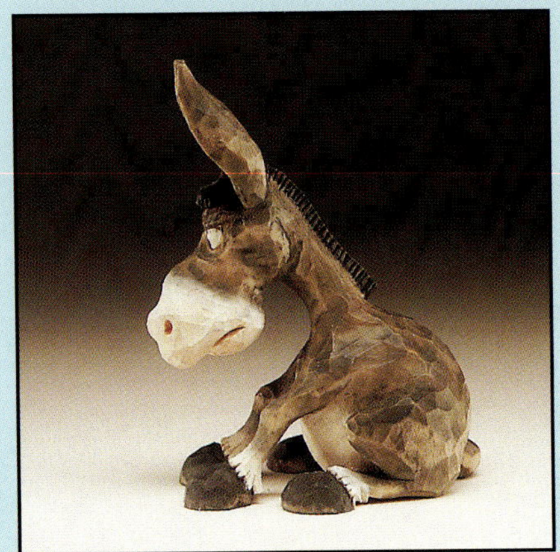

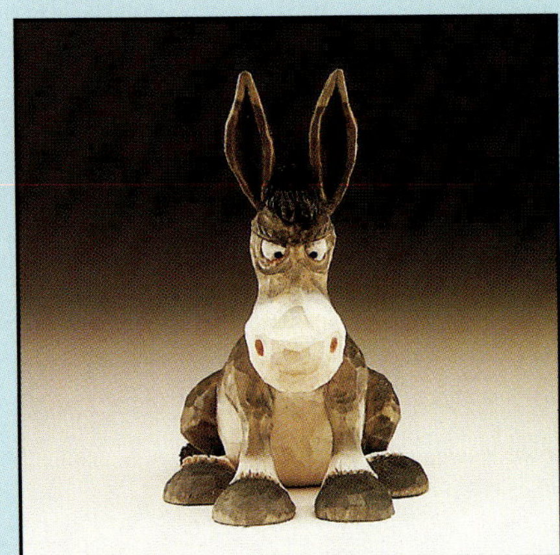

Donkeys make good caricature subjects. Their features are easy to exaggerate. Lazy Jack was made even more hilarious by having him in a sitting position.

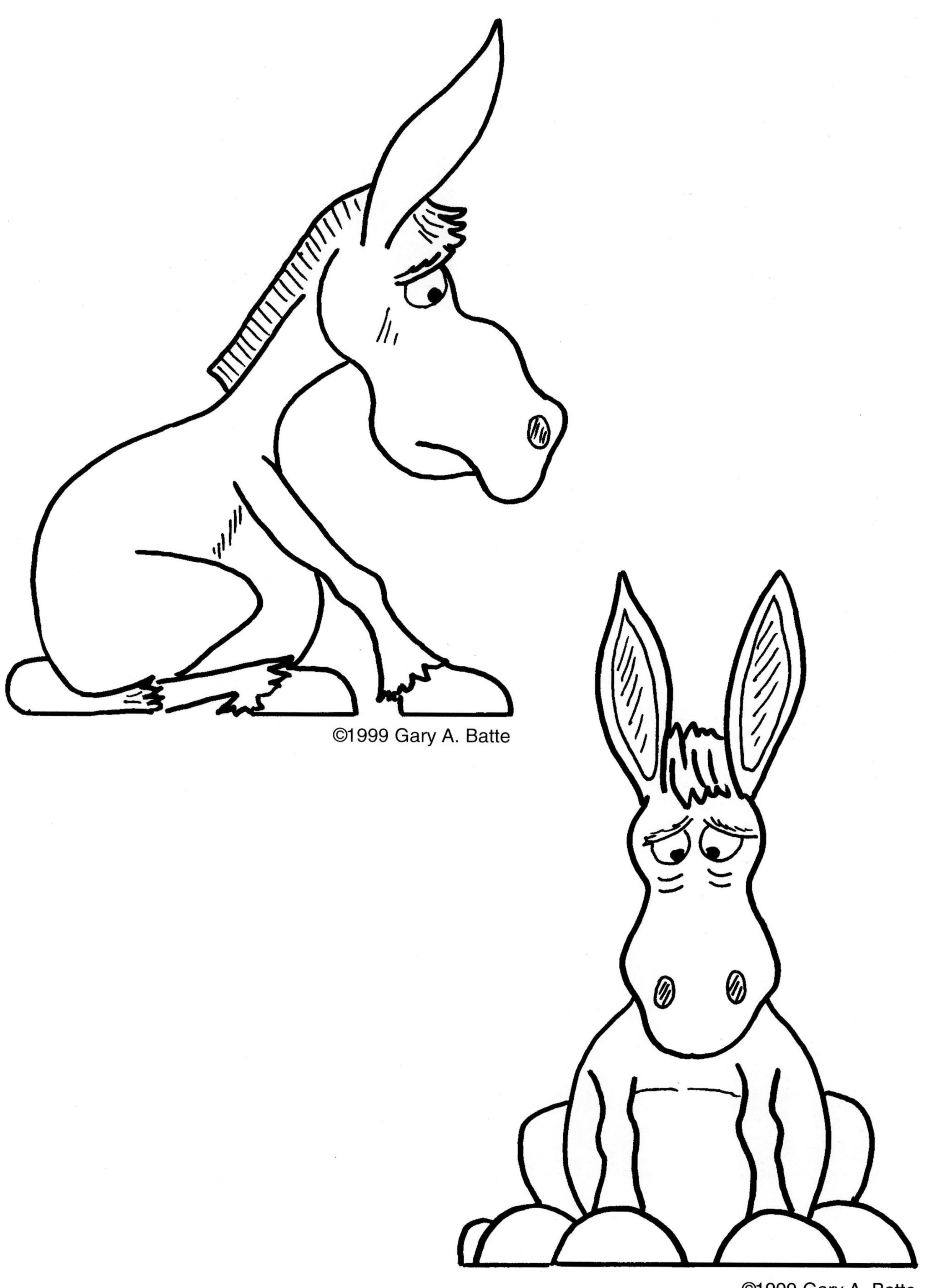

Donkeys have a way of looking funny even if they're not caricatures. Distortion of their features make them even more hilarious and fun to carve. Jack is a rather lazy donkey, which is probably why he's sitting on his rear end. He has large feet, long ears, a big snout and goofy eyes.

ROUGHING OUT

To carve Lazy Jack, a block of wood $3^1/4$ inches thick by 4 inches wide by $5^1/8$ inches long is required. The grain should run with the $5^1/8$-inch length. Round Jack's back and neck, leaving about a $^1/8$-inch width along the top of the neck for the mane. Remove some wood from between and behind the front legs and feet, back to the belly. When completed, the legs will be fragile, so save the final carving of them until last. Mark the bottom of each foot. Carve some of the surplus from outside each front leg and foot.

Remove surplus from the top and side of each hind leg and foot, stopping at the end of the tail which lies alongside the right leg. Round Jack's bottom and carve the tail to curve around the bottom. Leave about a $^1/4$-inch thickness for the tail. Round the belly, feet and legs.

Remove surplus wood from the sides of Jack's head and nose. Mark the jawline and remove wood from behind the jaw with a 3 mm veiner. Round the jawline with a knife. Round the nose and head, leaving wood for the hair to extend over the forehead. Remove surplus

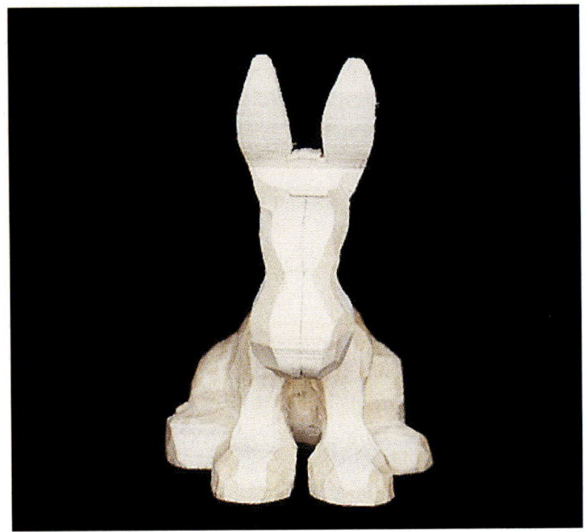

Front view, roughed out

wood from the front and back of each ear, extending to the point of their attachment on each side of the head.

DETAIL CARVING

Shape Jack's ears and remove wood from the inside of the ears with a veiner or a gouge. Use a knife to remove wood from the corners.

Continue shaping the nose and carve the nostrils with a veiner. Carve the mouth. When carving the eyes, mark the droopy brows first; then carve the eye sockets below the brows, leaving a mound in the center for the eyeball. Carve the eye as described in the Sweet Pea project.

Finish carving the legs and the feet. Carve the separation between the hips and the belly. Shape each hoof and carve the hairline just above the hoof. First make a stop cut around the leg along the hair line; then use a v-tool or

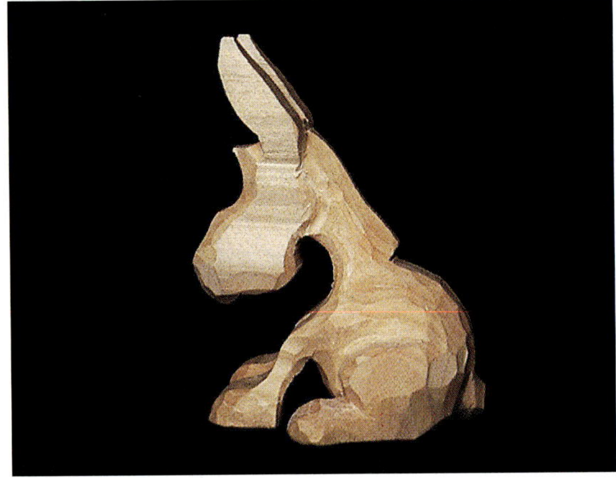

Side view, roughed out

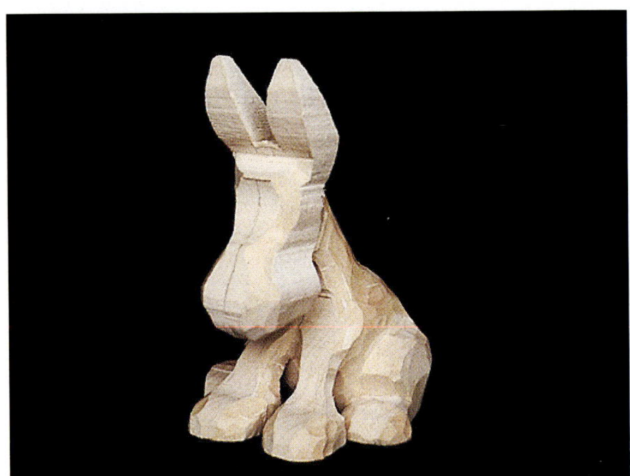

Angle view, roughed out

knife to remove a series of small wedges along the stop cut. Carve along each side of the mane with a gouge or veiner, leaving the mane about 1/4 inch long. Carve the hair on the mane, tail and brows with a v-tool.

PAINTING AND FINISHING

Paint the body, except for the nose, belly and lower part of the legs, with a very thin black wash to give Jack a gray look. The belly, nose, eyeball and lower part of each leg are white. Blend the white where it meets the gray with a dry brush while the gray is still wet. Do a small area at a time. The insides of the ears are raw umber mixed with a very small amount of black. The nostrils and lips are cadmium red light mixed with raw umber. The hooves, the mane and the end of the tail are black. Paint a black dot on each eyeball. Apply crimson red light to the lower inside of the eyelids with a small brush. Seal the piece with antiquing.

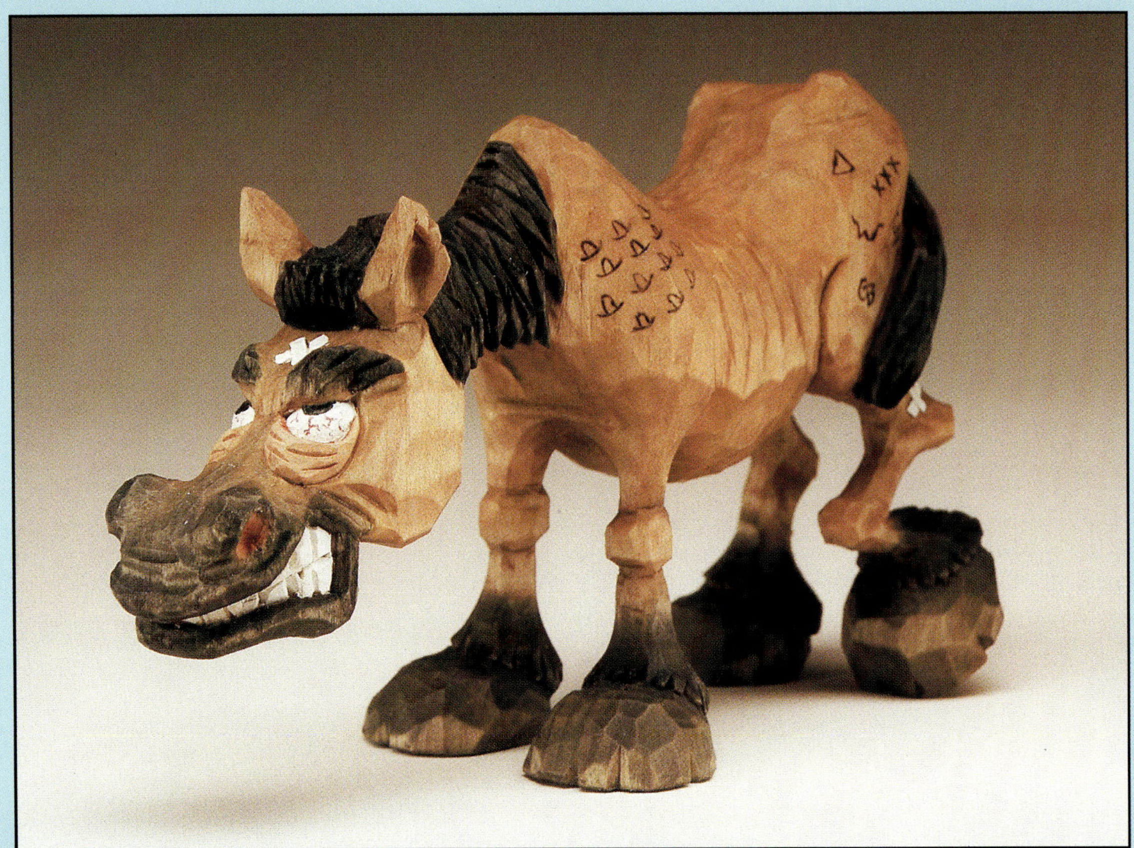

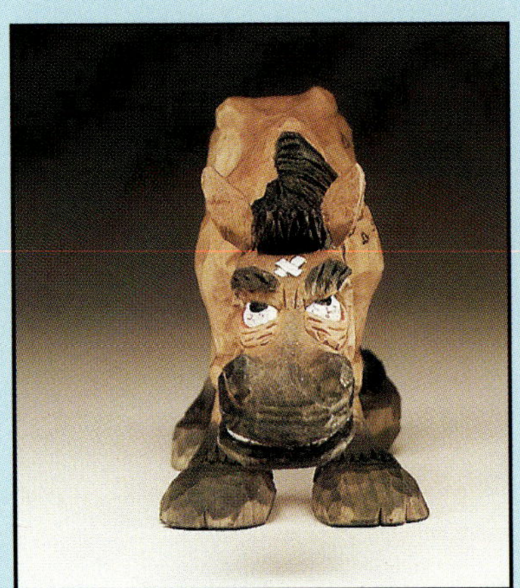

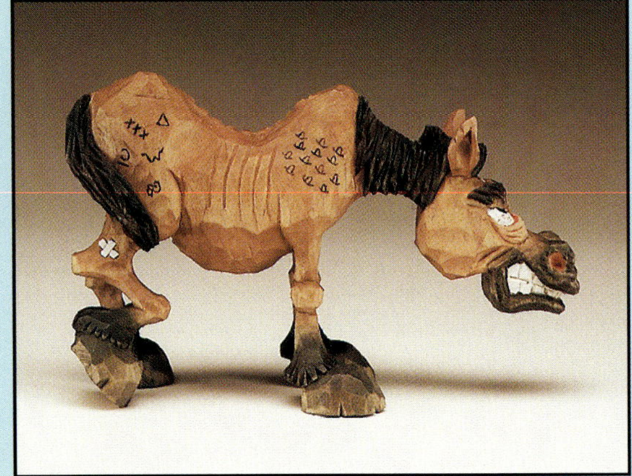

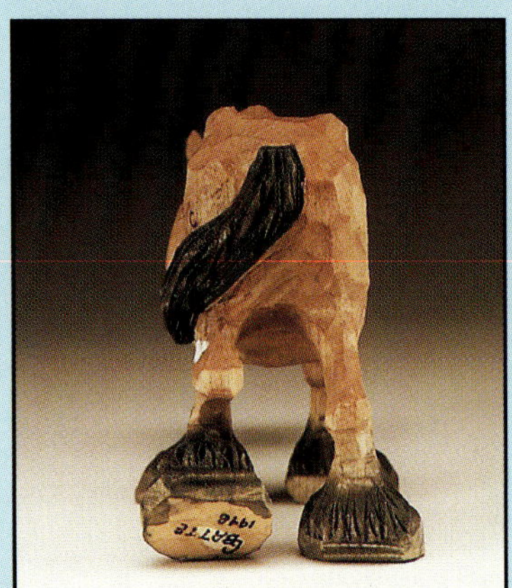

Dynamite has been through the rodeo wars, and it appears that he has won most of them. Carving the left hind leg is a little tricky. Because the grain runs vertically, it is easy to break. For his appearance to live up to his name, he must be given a really mean, killer look.

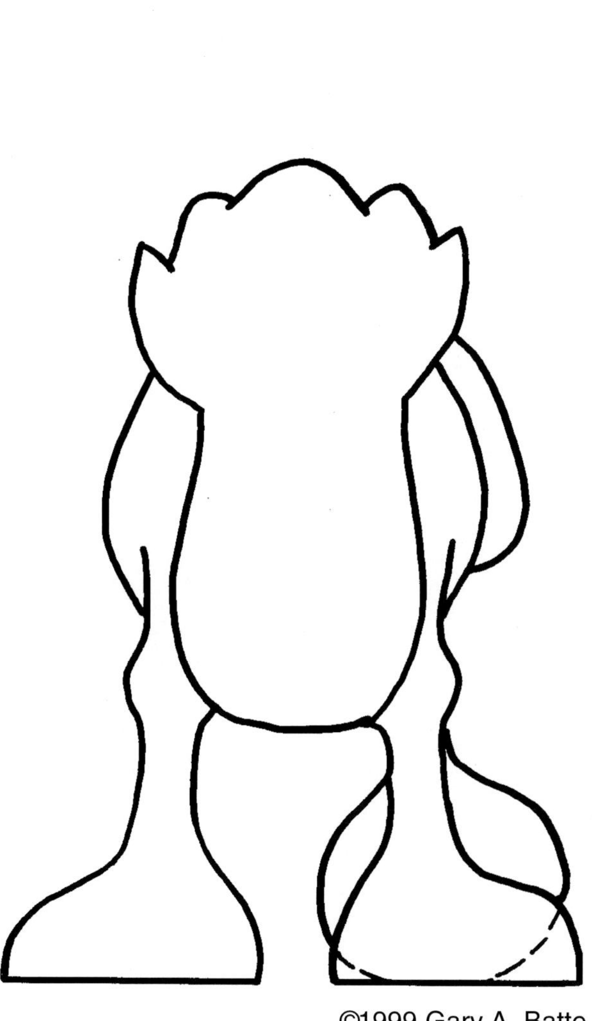

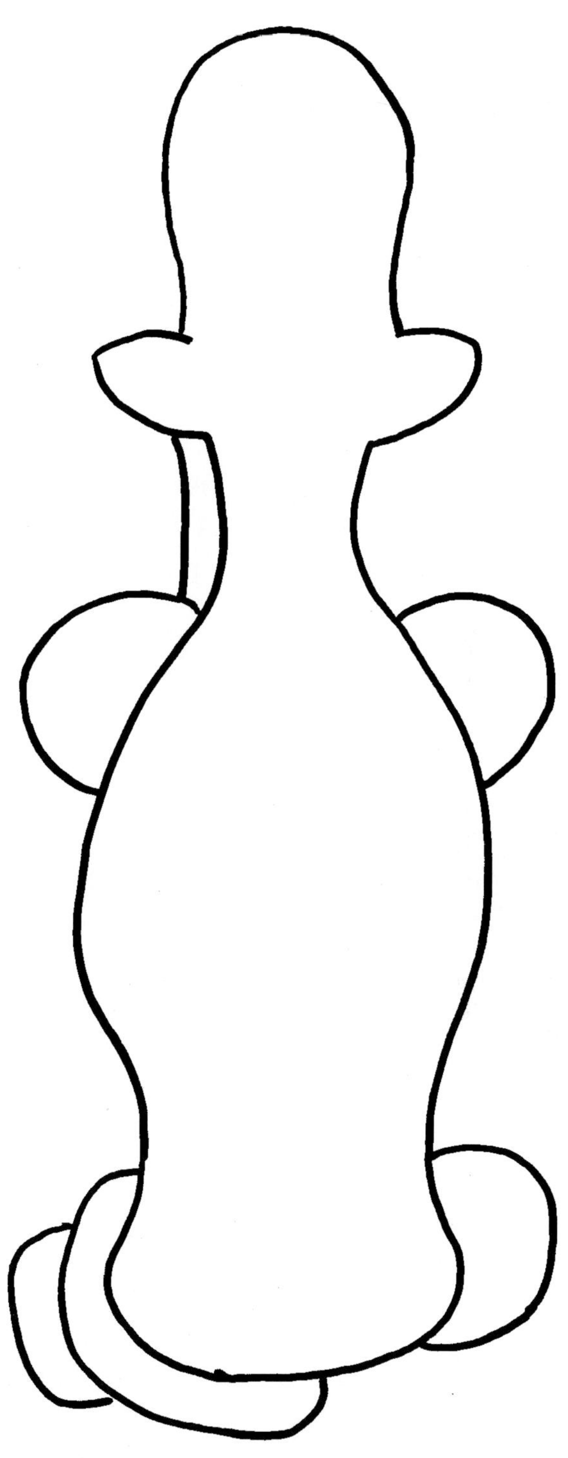

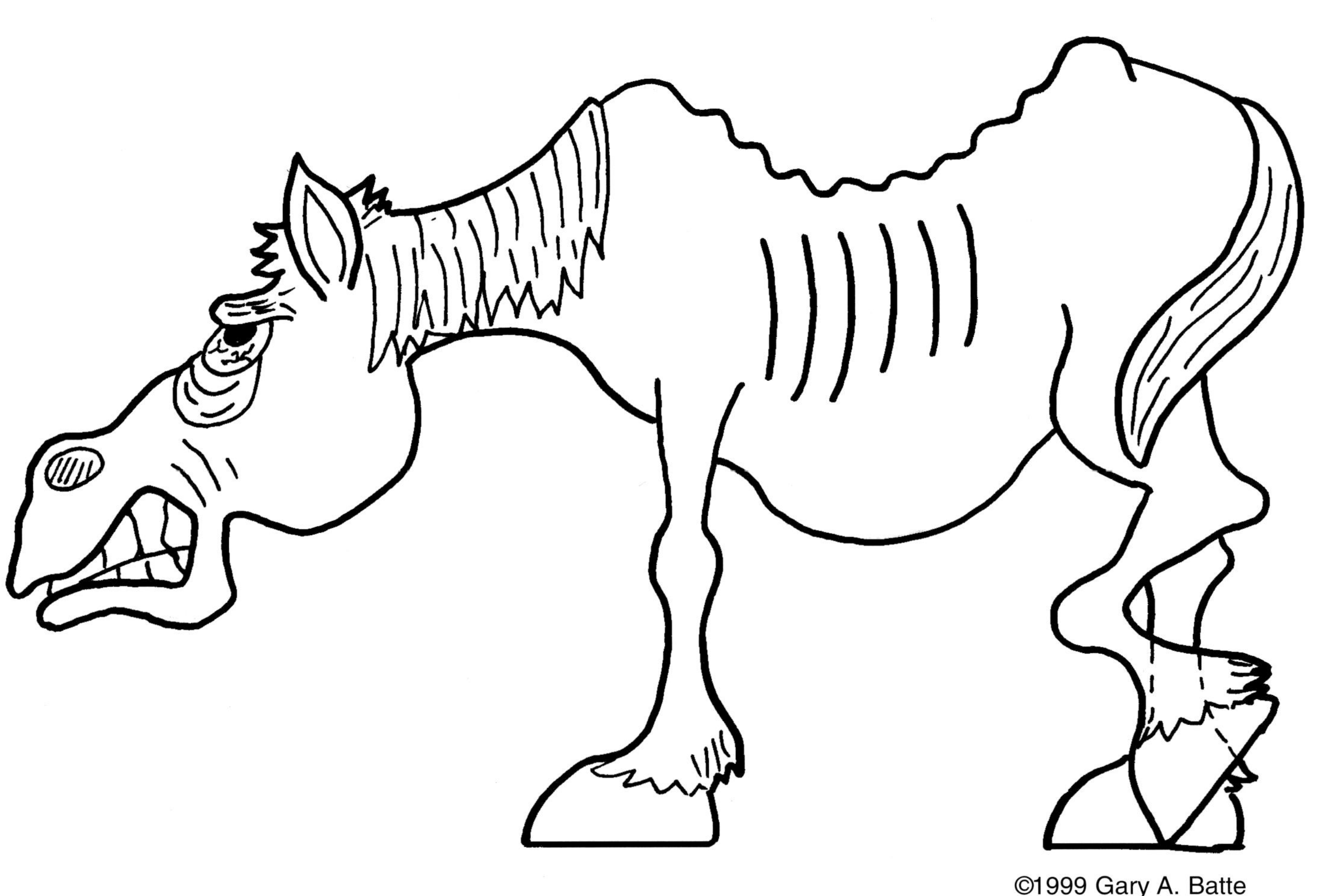

Dynamite is a rodeo bronc that's obviously seen better days. The hat tally on his shoulder shows that he is accustomed to retiring cowboys from their profession. Regardless of mileage, Dynamite still has that "killer" look in his eye. It's his raw-boned, broken-down condition and mean personality that's to be captured in this carving. Larger-than-normal feet and head add to the character.

ROUGHING OUT

Bandsawing Dynamite is done a little differently from previous projects. Begin with a piece of wood 3 inches thick by $4^1/_2$ inches wide by $7^1/_4$ inches long. Bandsaw the side view first, then the top view. Round his belly and back, leaving a ridge of wood for the backbone. Remove surplus from the sides of the neck and head. Round the head, nose, neck, shoulders and rump, leaving wood for the tail and mane. The hip bones and backbone are left prominent. Mark the side and front views of the feet, the legs and the bottoms of the feet. Since the left foot is tilted, remove about two-thirds of the surplus from the bottom, front, sides and between the legs. This job is first made easier by drilling a series of holes between the legs; then using a gouge and knife to finish. Care must be given to proper positioning of the left leg and foot. Legs and feet can now be rounded and shaped. Save final carving of the left leg and foot until the very last to minimize chance of breakage.

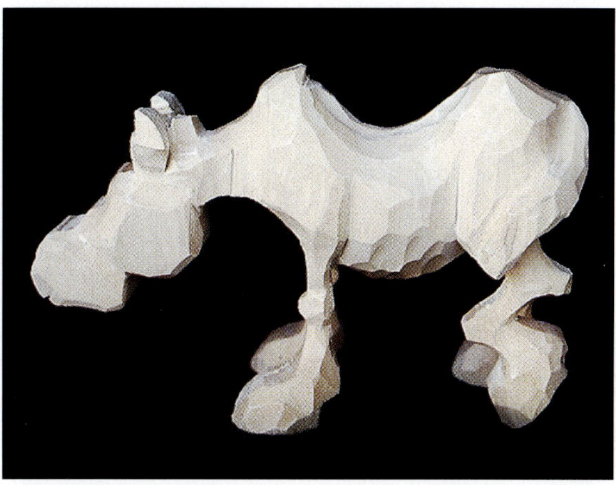

Side view, roughed out

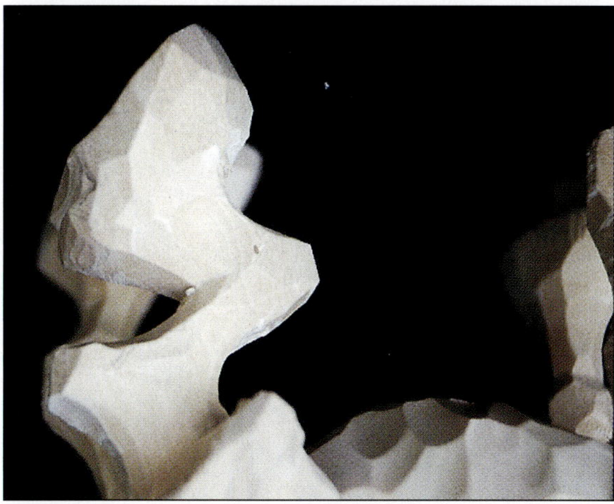

Left hind leg, roughed out

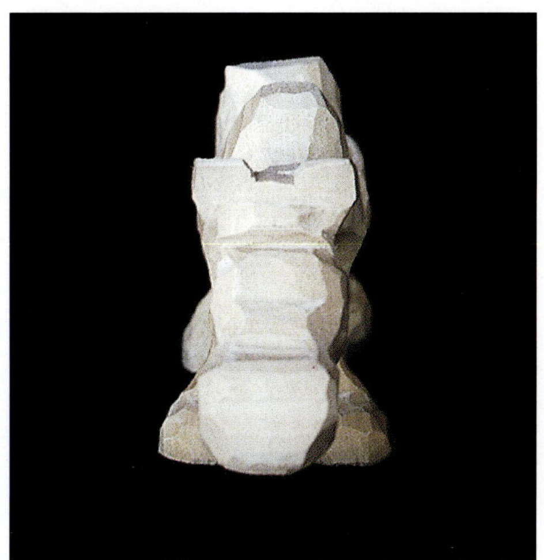

Front view, roughed out

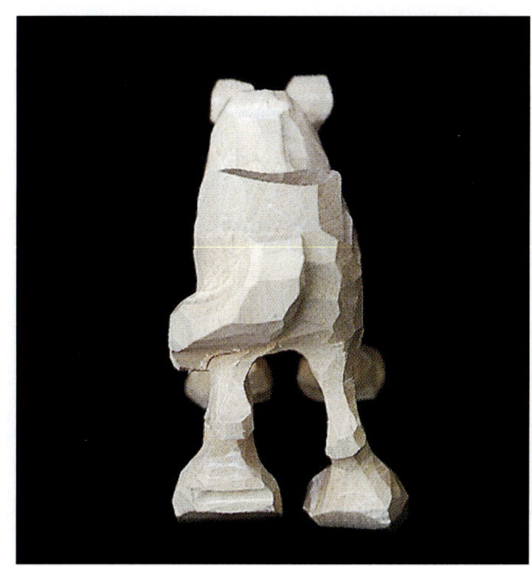

Back view, roughed out

Do some preliminary shaping of the head and ears.

DETAIL CARVING

Finish shaping Dynamite's nose and carve the nostrils with 5 mm veiner; then remove wood from around the outside of each nostril to make them stand out. Make a knife stop cut along the lip lines; then remove wood inside where the teeth will be. Round the lips and carve the teeth with a v-tool and a knife. The eyes will add to the "killer" look. Create "mean" eyebrows by removing wood below them with a 5 mm veiner. Carve around the eye, including the bag underneath, and round the eyeball. Carve wrinkles below the eyes with a v-tool. After shaping the ears with a knife, hollow them out with a 5 mm veiner and knife. Carve the hair on the mane and tail with a 4 mm v-tool. Also carve the ribs with the 4 mm v-tool and round the edges of the cuts with a knife. A 3 mm veiner is used to create ridges across the backbone. Carve the hairline around the lower leg just above the hoof as described in the "Lazy Jack" project. Cut a few notches in each hoof to complete the look of a worn-out rodeo bronc.

PAINTING AND FINISHING

Dynamite's body is painted with a very thin wash of dark brown. The mane and tail are black. The hooves are a thinner black wash. The teeth and eyeballs are white. Only one-half of the black portion of the eye can be seen below the brow. The eyelids are red. A fine-tipped red ink pen was used to make the squiggly lines for blood shot eyeballs. The nostrils are flesh mixed with cadmium red light. Hats and brands are applied with a woodburner or black-brown paint and the carving is antiqued.

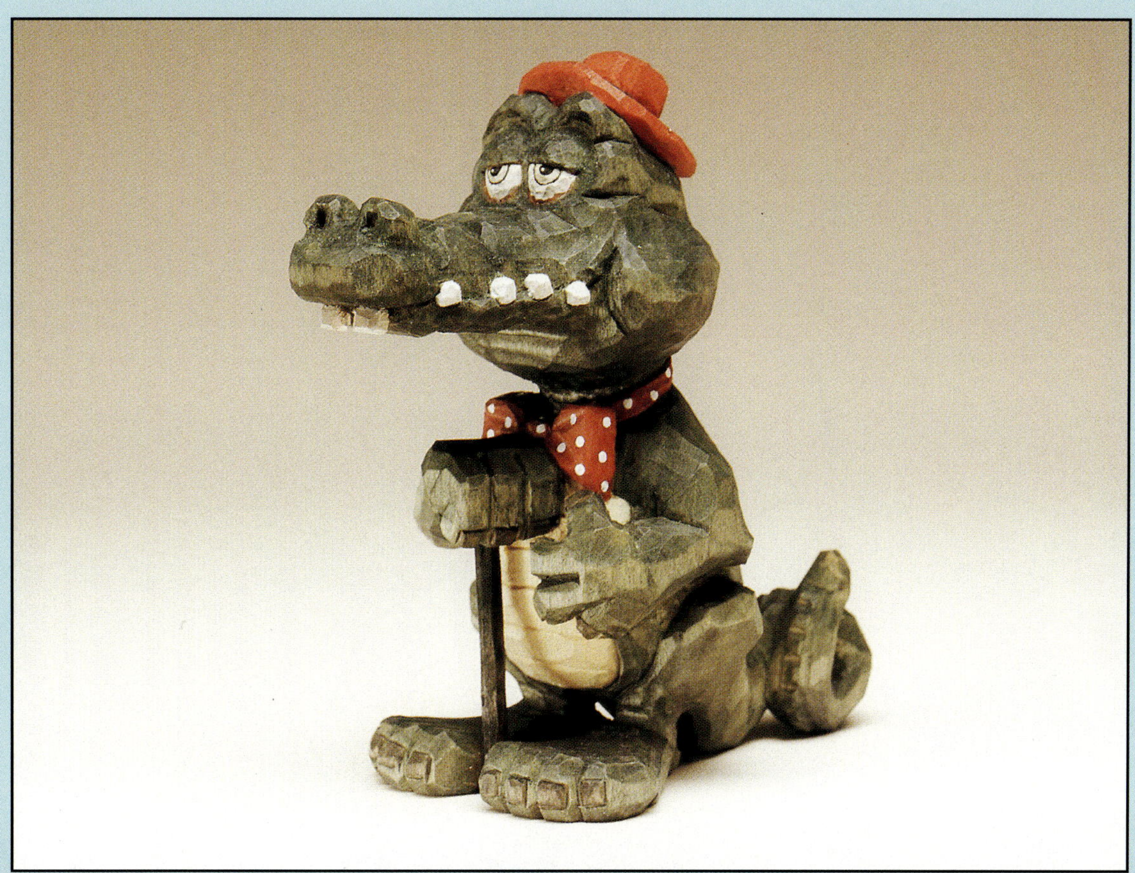

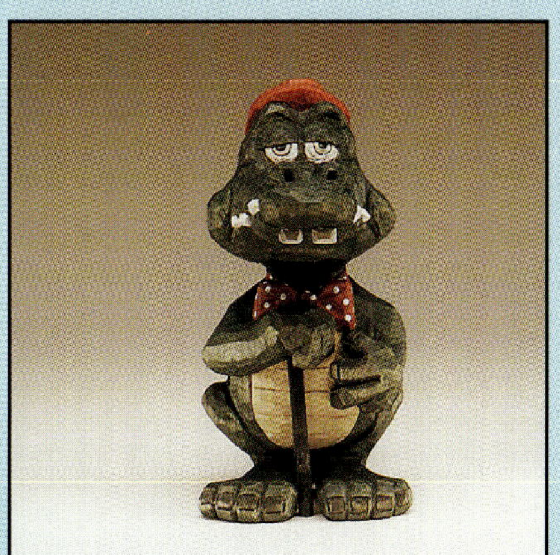

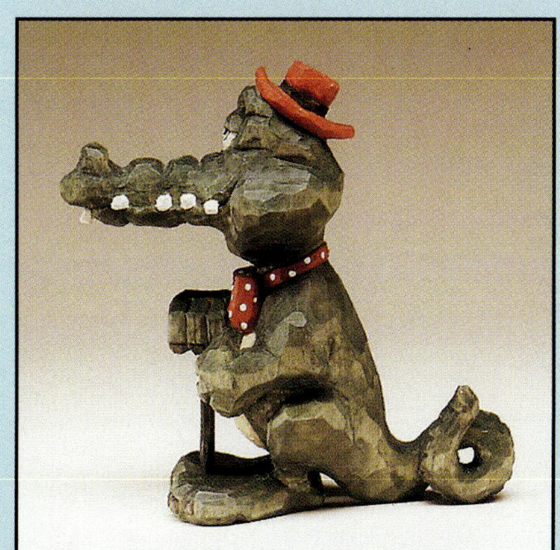

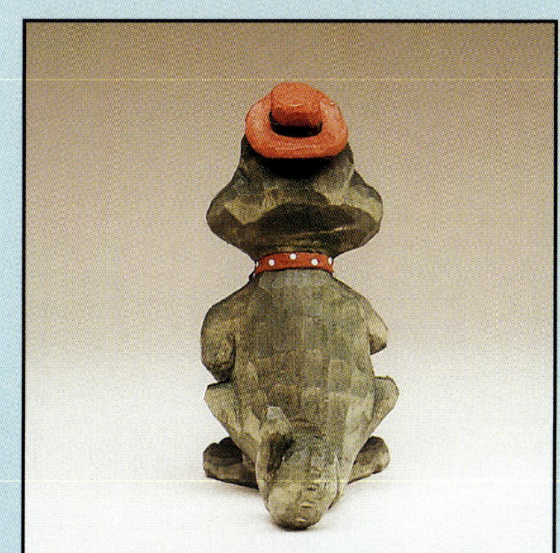

A caricature alligator was included because I haven't seen any in other carving books. It also makes an interesting subject to caricaturize. Al tries to look more sophisticated than he really is.

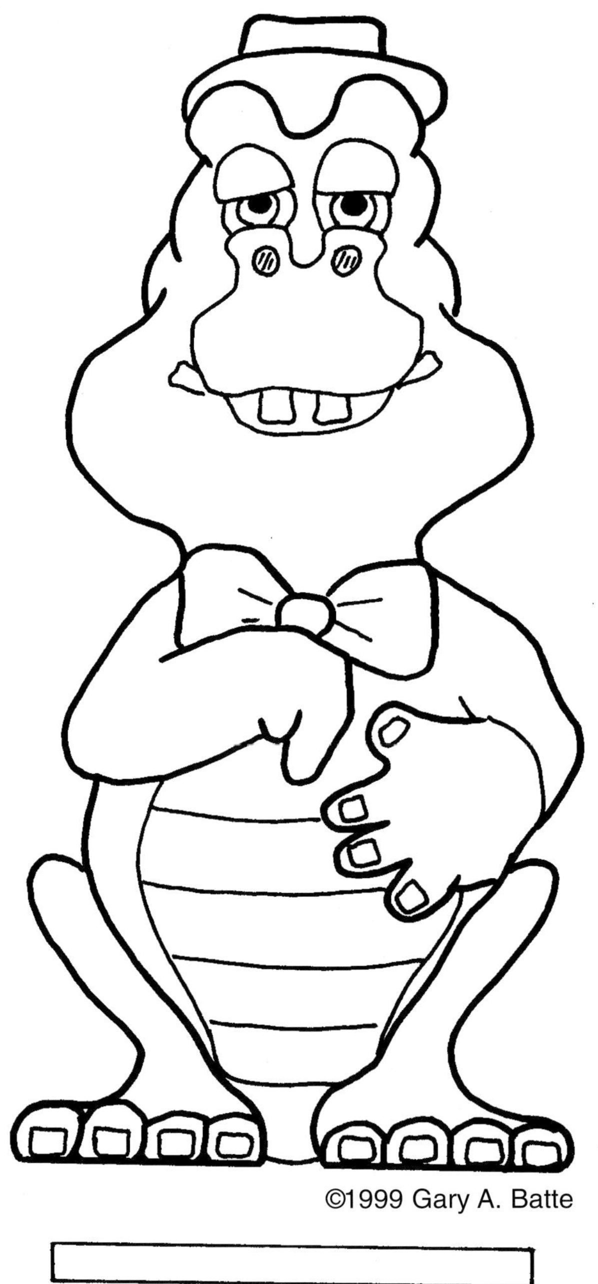

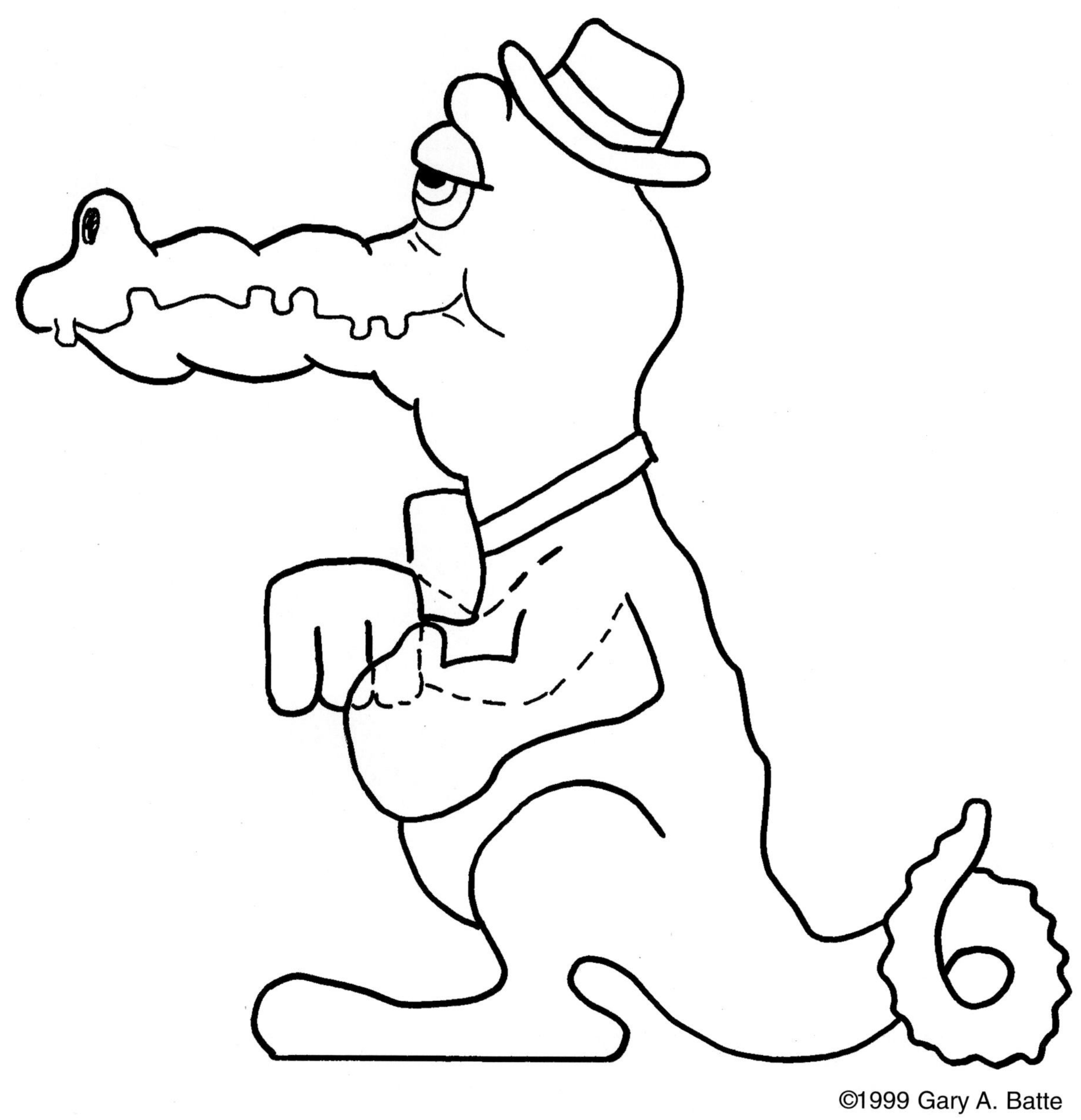

Instead of carving a plain old gator, I decided to spiff this one up a bit by adding a hat, bow tie and cane. Besides, this puts a little more challenge into the piece.

ROUGHOUT

The carving, as designed, requires a piece of wood 2 7/8 inches thick by 6 inches wide by 6 inches long. The grain runs the vertical 6-inch length.

Bandsaw the side and front views. Mark the bottom view of the feet and a 1 3/8 inch width for the tail. Remove surplus wood from each side of Al's tail, feet and snout. Leave the tail about 1 3/8 inches wide to allow for the curl.

Mark the front view. Remove excess wood from above and below the right foreleg and the foot, being careful to leave wood for the hind leg below it. The foreleg is angled across the chest. When carving wood from the top of the foot, be sure to stop at the front of the bow tie. Remove surplus from behind both the right front and right back legs and round the belly just below the right foot. Round the right side of the back down to the tail.

The left legs and left side of the belly will be carved similar to the right side, except for the different positioning of the foreleg and the foot. Now, round the rest of the body, neck and snout, leaving wood for the teeth and nostrils.

Shape the front and the outside of Al's back feet. Carve between the feet, back to the tail, using veiners and gouges. Drill a 1/4-inch hole at the curl of the tail. Carve that part of the tail that extends upward first. Finish rounding the

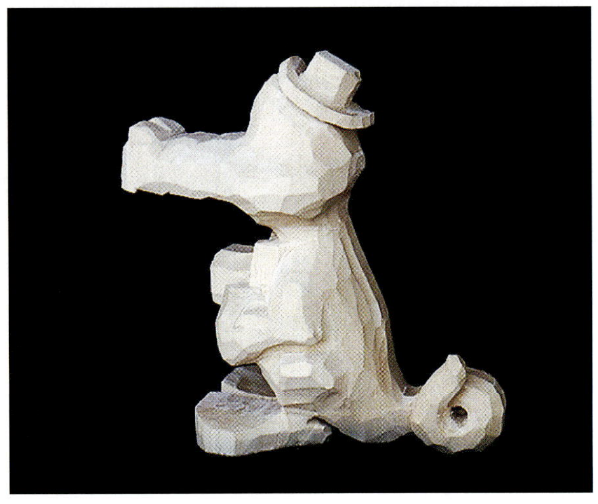

Side view, roughed out

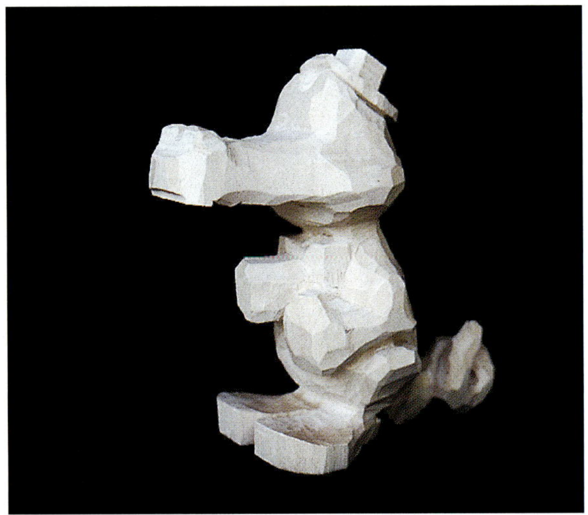

Angle view, roughed out

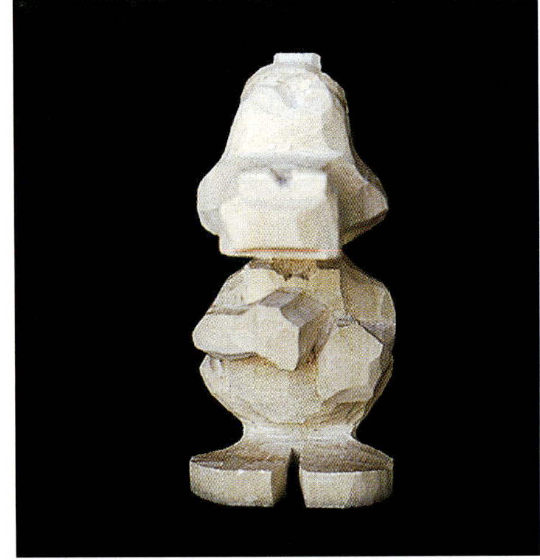

Front view, roughed out

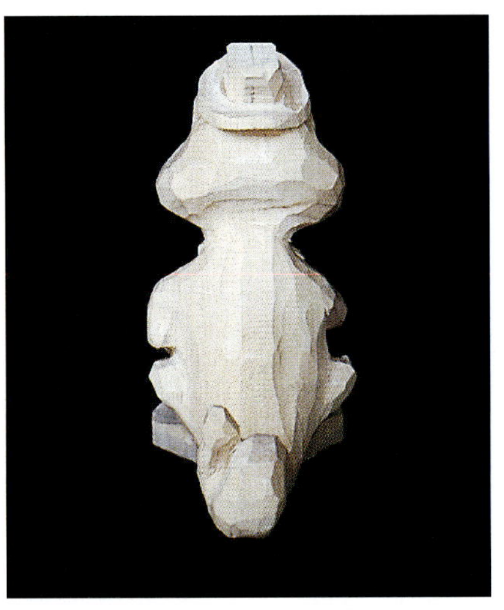

Back view, roughed out

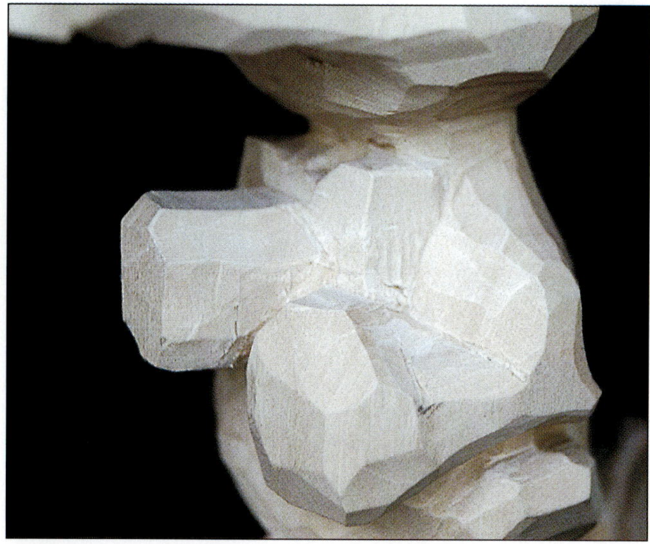

Forelegs and bow tie, roughed out

tail, leaving a 1/8-wide ridge along the top side.

Round the hat brim and remove some wood from under the edges. Carve the crown. Remove surplus wood from the sides and the top of the bow tie.

DETAIL CARVING

Carve the toe separations with 4 mm v-tool. Also use a 2 mm veiner to carve between the toes on the left front foot.

Round the edges of the bow tie and round the knot with a knife tip. Creases adjacent to the knot are carved with a v-tool. Carve the tie around Al's neck.

Complete shaping and rounding the tail. Use a 2 mm veiner to make a series of cuts across the ridge on the tail.

Shape Al's head and nose. Mark the mouth line and the teeth. Carve the teeth with a 3 mm veiner and a knife. Remove surplus wood from the side of the snout above the teeth with a #7 – 8 mm gouge.

The eyes are carved in the same manner as in the Sweet Pea project. Carve the nostrils with a 3 mm veiner, making the first cut from the top to the bottom to avoid splitting the wood. Then make a second cut at the bottom to remove the wood from the nostril.

Finish rounding the tail and make a series of cuts across the ridge with a 2 mm gouge. The hide on Al's back needs to be rough. Create a gator look by making several shallow cuts with a #3 – 14 mm fishtail gouge. Practice making these cuts on a scrap piece of wood first.

Carve a band on the hat.

The cane is 2 1/2 inches long and about 3/16 inch in diameter. After carving, hold the cane in place and mark the location of the upper end where it meets the underside of the foot. Use a small gouge or veiner to drill a 1/4-inch-deep hole in the bottom side of the foot where the cane will be inserted.

PAINTING AND FINISHING

The body is black-green, except for the belly, which is parchment. The bow tie is napthol red light mixed with a small amount of raw umber to tone it down. The white dots are made by cutting off the end of a round toothpick and dipping it into undiluted paint straight from the bottle. The hat is the same red/raw umber mixture, and the band is black. The eyeballs and the teeth are white. The irises are raw umber, and the pupils are black with white highlight dots. The cane and nails are black. The insides of the nostrils are raw umber. Apply antiquing and wipe off the excess. Glue the cane in place.

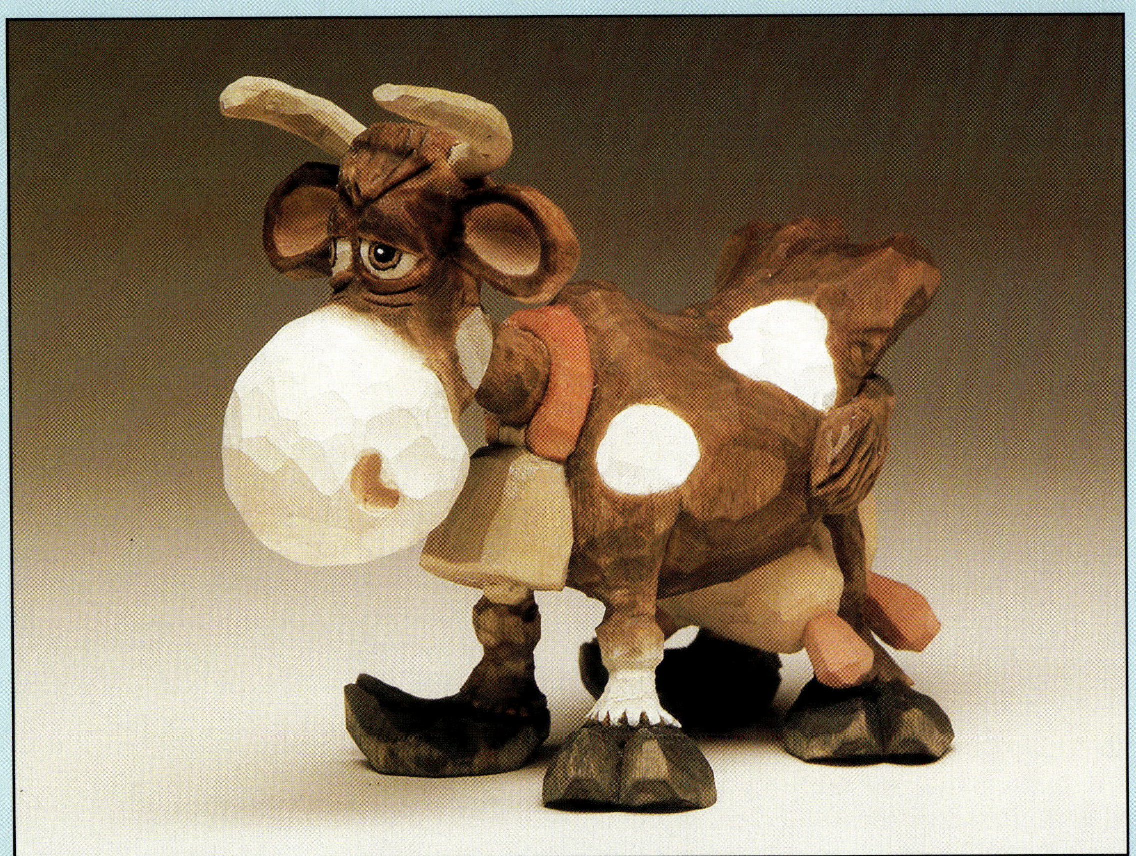

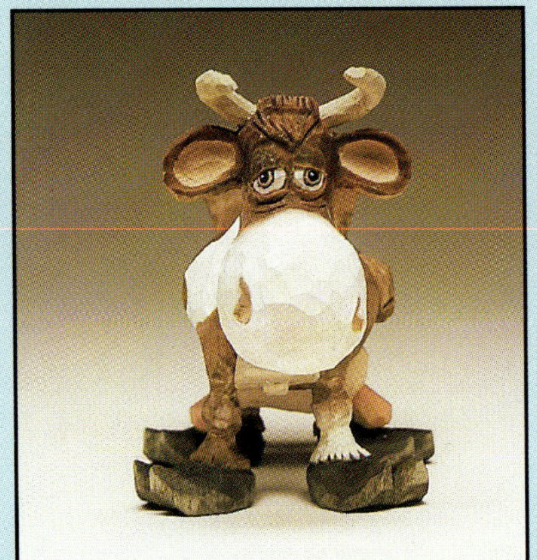

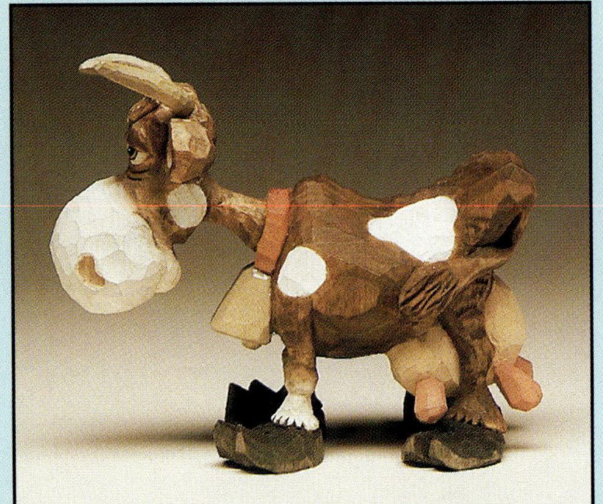

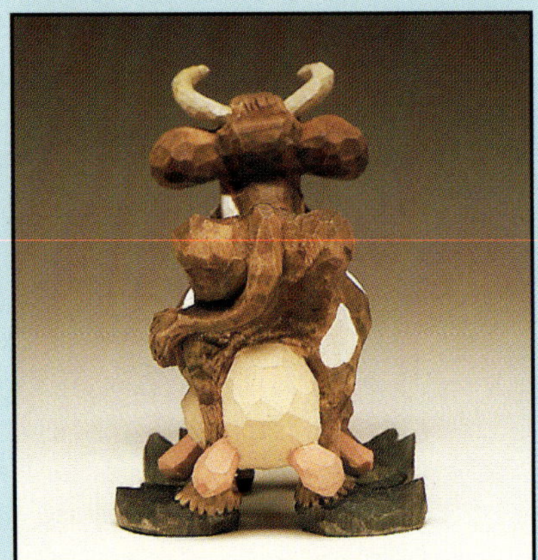

Buttercup is one of the most difficult and challenging projects in this book. It also presents a very funny caricature carving. For the less experienced, I recommend carving some of the earlier projects before tackling this one.

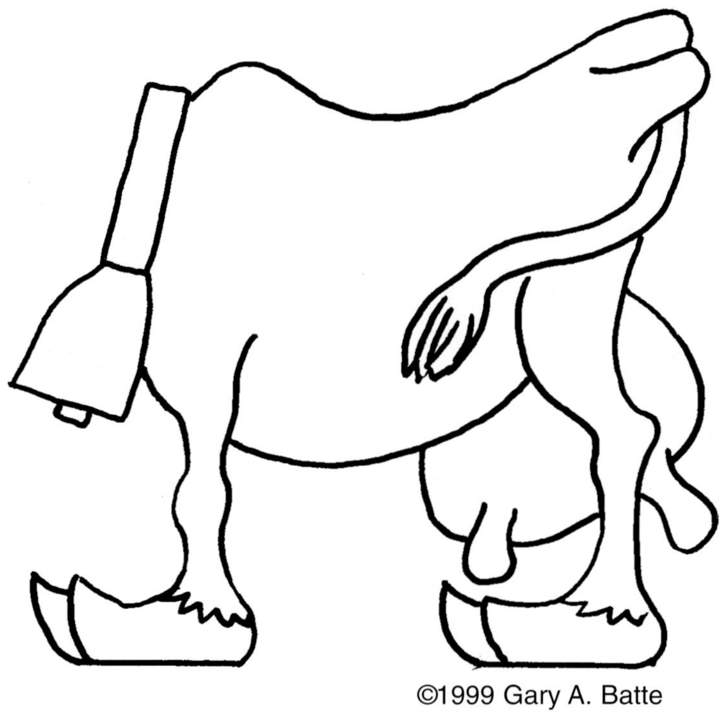

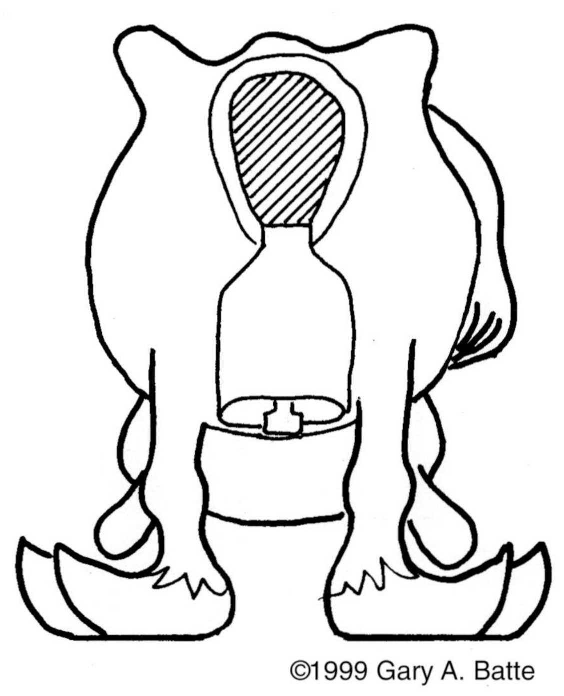

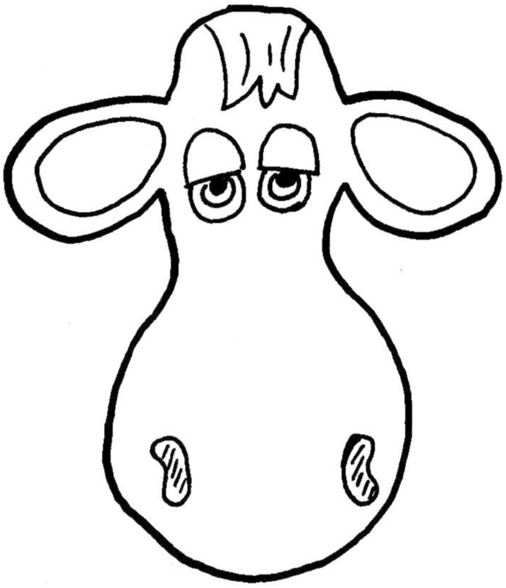

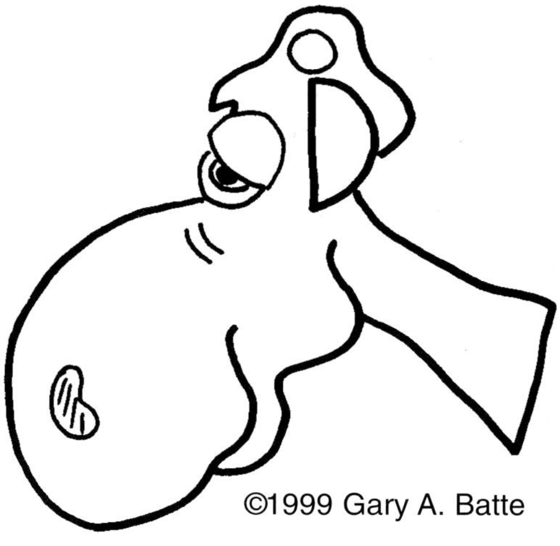

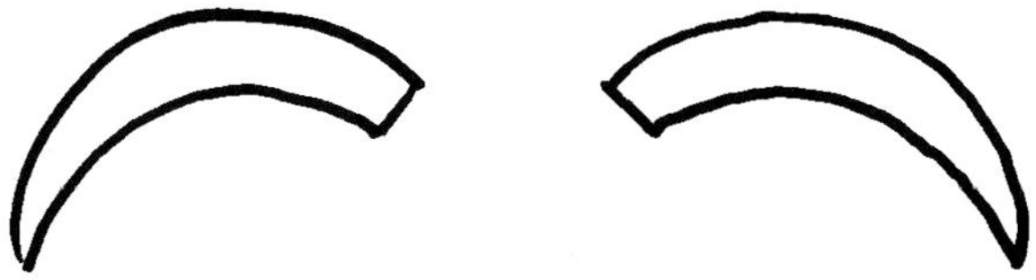

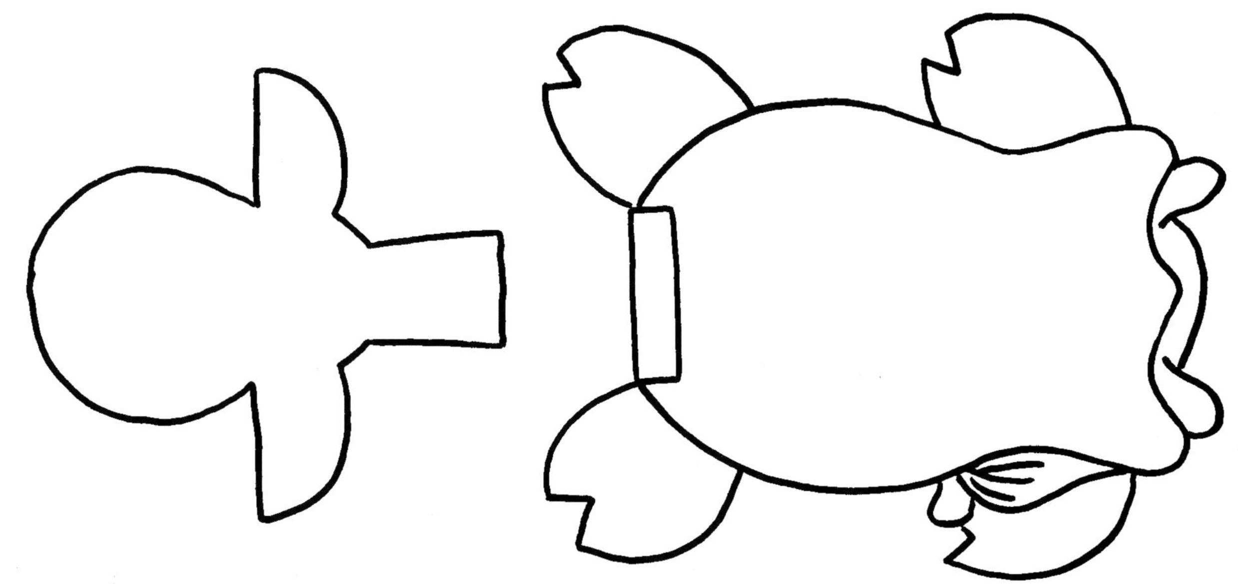

Buttercup is the "Queen of Moo." As you can see, she is "udderly" tops in the milk department. To create a funny cow caricature, Buttercup's udder is overemphasized, and she has a skinny neck, large nose and goofy eyes. The feet are oversized and turn upward on the ends. The hip bones are very prominent. Because Buttercup's neck would be subject to easy breakage if carved all in one piece, the head and horns are each carved separately.

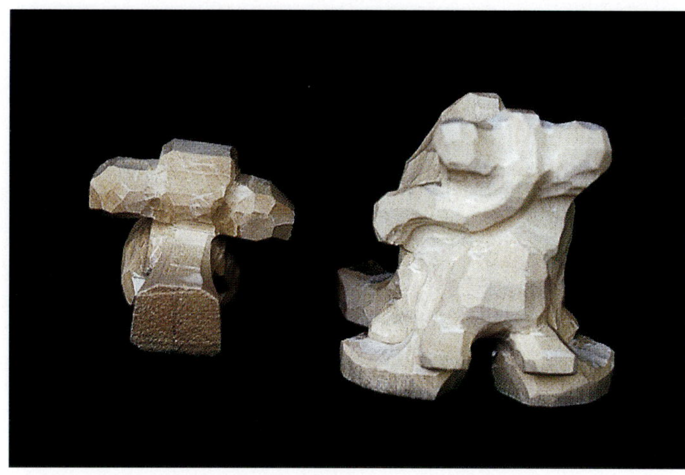

Back view of head and body, roughed out

ROUGHING OUT

A block of wood 3 inches thick by 3 1/2 inches wide by 4 3/4 inches long is required for Buttercup's body. The grain runs the 3 1/2-inch width. Bandsaw the side view first; then the top view. Mark the tail and the underside of the feet. Remove the surplus wood from around the legs and shoulders. Round the belly, back and rump, leaving wood for the feet, bell, collar and udder. When rounding the rump, leave the tail curved around the rump and leave wood protruding for the hip bones.

For the head, a block of wood 2 3/8 inches thick by 2 3/8 inches wide by 2 3/4 inches long is needed. Turn the pattern so that the grain will run in the same direction as the neck. Saw out the side view. Remove surplus wood from the sides of the neck, head and nose, leaving the full 2 3/8 inches width for the ears. Round the nose, back of the head and the neck.

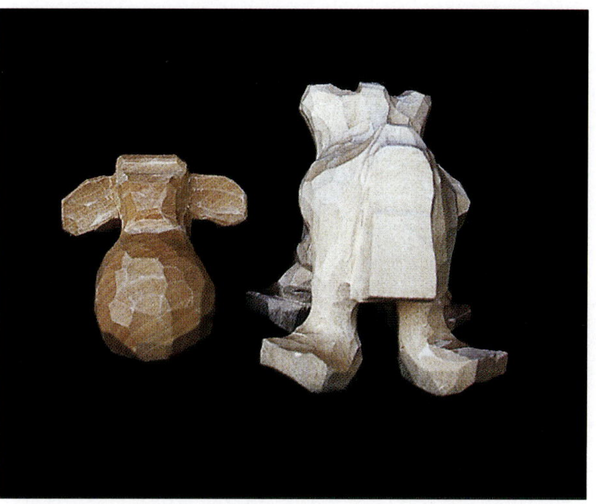

Front view of head and body, roughed out

DETAIL CARVING

Finish shaping Buttercup's nose and head. Leave some wood for the hair that hangs on the forehead. Remove surplus wood from behind the

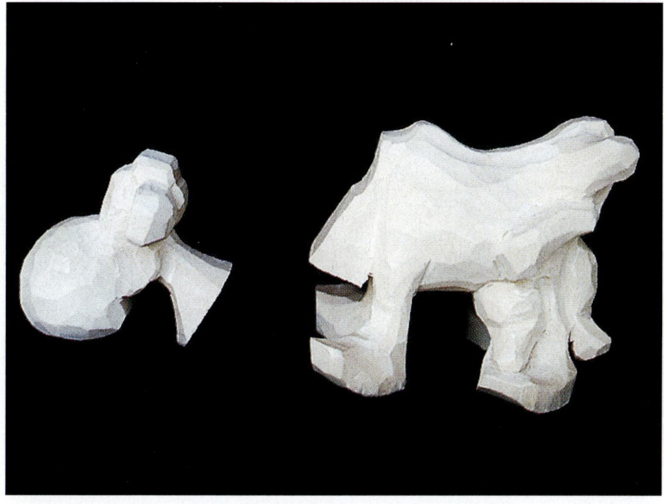

Side view of head and body, roughed out

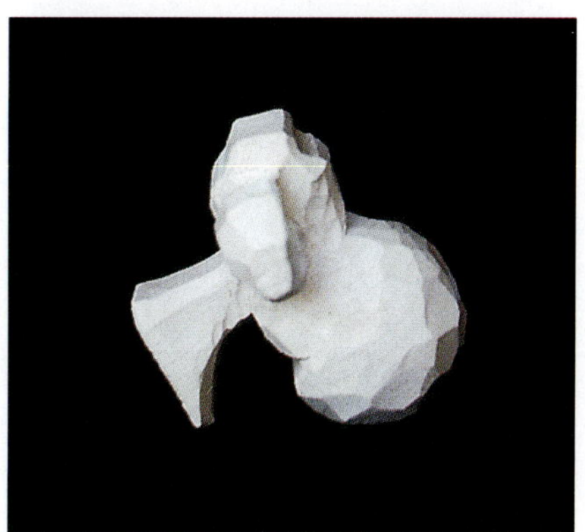

Side view of head, roughed out

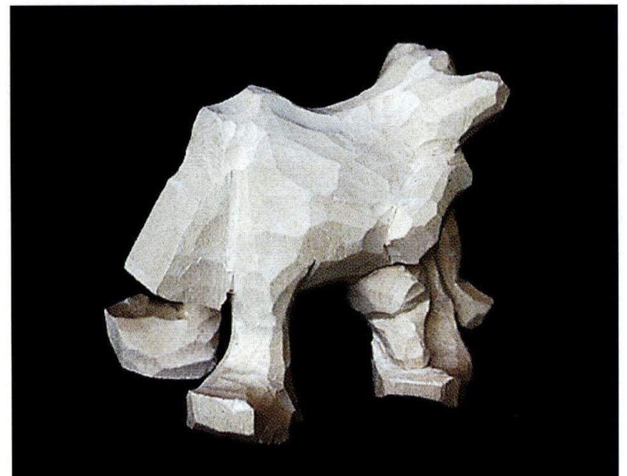

Angle view of body, roughed out

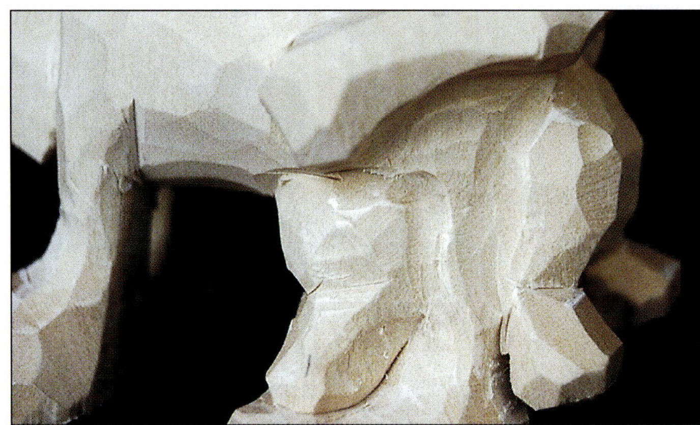

Side view udder, roughed out

ears and carve the jawline. Shape the ears.

Hollow out the ears and nostrils with veiners and gouges. Carve the mouth. Refer to the Sweet Pea project for carving the eyes. Carve the horns separately.

Use a 5 mm veiner to remove wood along each side of the tail and between the base of the tail and the hip bones. Carve the hip bones so that they protrude outward at an angle.

Mark the bottoms of the feet and shape them with a knife. Turn them up on the ends. Carve the cleft in each hoof with a knife and a v-tool. Carve separations between the udder and back legs and feet. Use veiners, gouges and a knife to shape the udder. Using the end of the neck piece as a pattern, mark the inside of the collar and hollow it out to a depth of 3/16 inch. Shape the bell, leaving a portion of the clapper showing.

Carve the hair on the end of the tail and on the top of head with a v-tool. Vary the cuts in length, depth and direction.

PAINTING AND FINISHING

Buttercup's body is burnt umber with white spots and a white nose. Paint the spots first. The nostrils and insides of the ears are flesh mixed with a small amount of raw umber. The eyeballs are white with raw umber irises and black pupils, with a white dot on each pupil. Cadmium red light was used for the inside of the eyelids. The hooves are black. Flesh is used for the udder. Make the teats darker by mixing cadmium red light with the flesh color. The horns are white mixed with raw umber. Paint the bell collar napthol red light mixed with raw umber. The bell is iridescent silver.

After painting, drill 7/32 holes for the horns and glue them in place. Glue the head and the neck piece into the bell collar. Finish with antiquing.

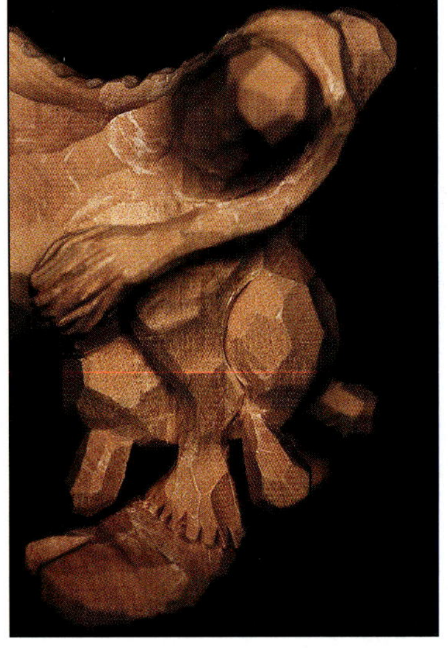

Udder, carving completed

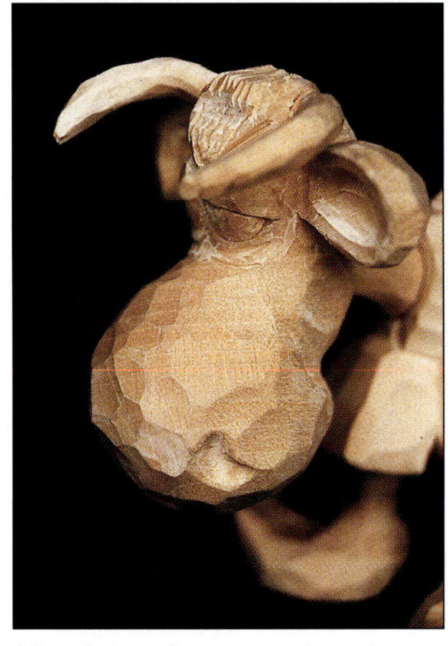

Head, carving completed

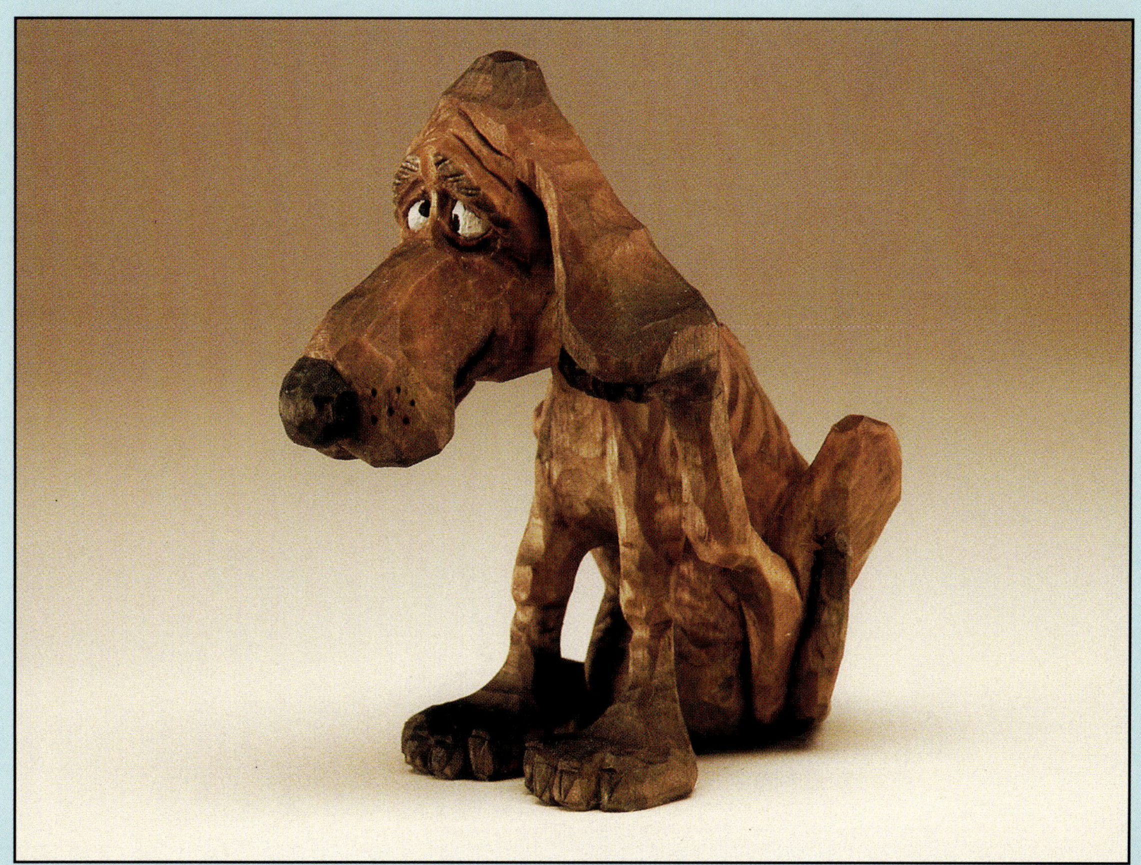

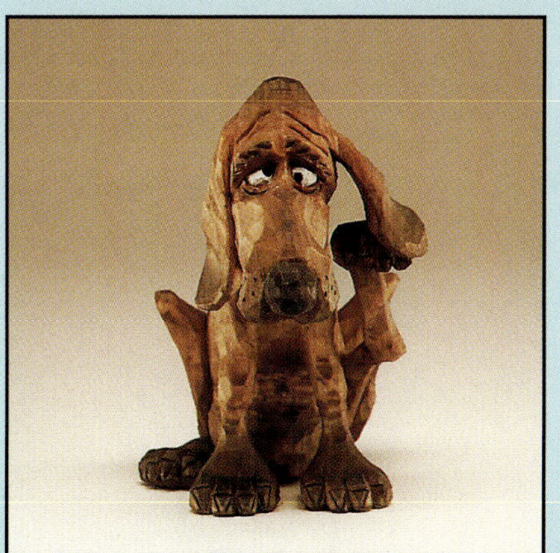

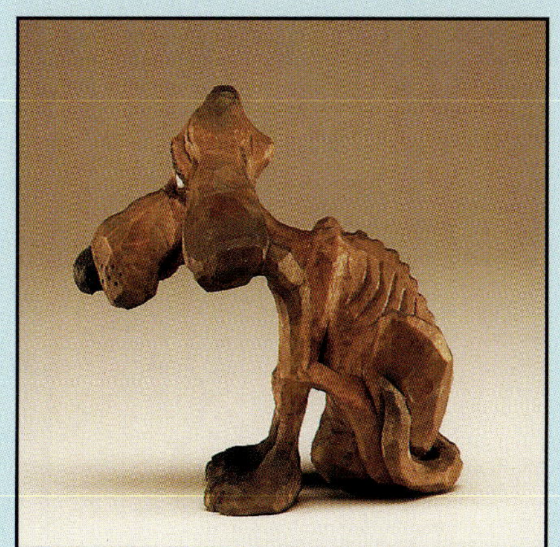

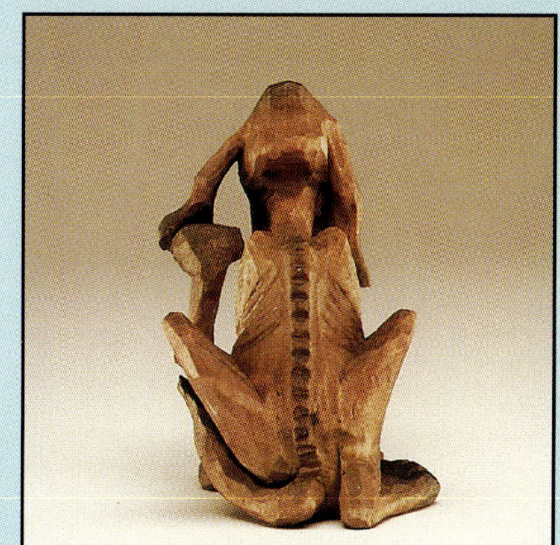

This hound dog makes a good caricature. When carving Flea-bitis, take care to make the cuts that emphasize his skinny, bony features. Note that the left hind leg is anchored to the underside of the ear for strength.

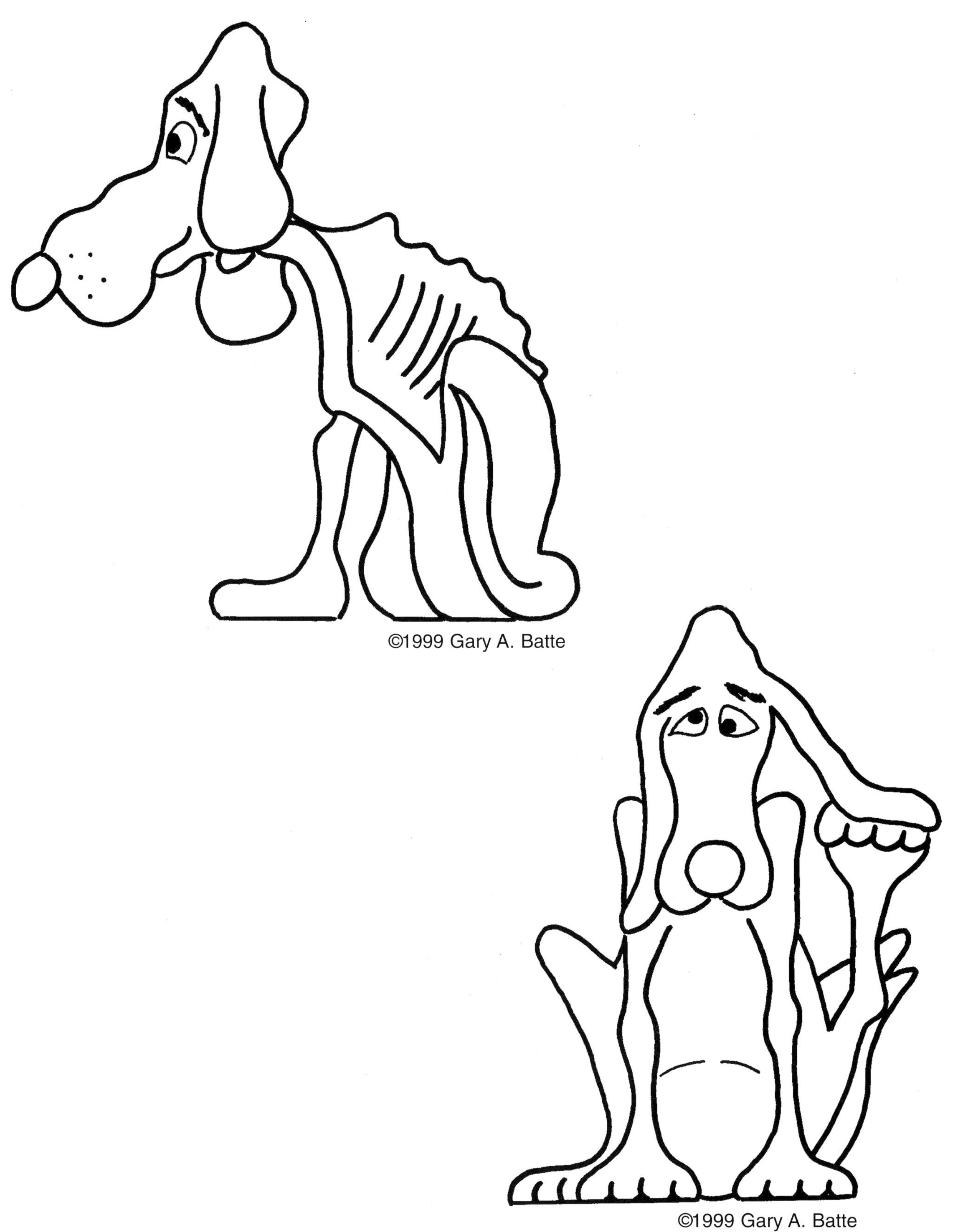

This old hound dog spends a lot of his time scratching fleas and other assorted bug-critters. He also spends a lot of his time running through the woods chasing varmints of all types, which might explain why he is so skinny.

ROUGHING OUT

Start with a block of wood 3 1/8 inches thick by 4 inches wide by 4 3/16 inches long. The grain must run with the 4 3/16-inch length.

Bandsaw the side and front views. Remove excess wood from each side of the front feet and legs up to the lower end of the right ear and to the bend in the raised left foot. Remove the surplus in front of and above the right back foot and leg. Round the right side of the belly. Carve excess wood from beneath the left paw and neck over to the right ear. Remove wood from above the extended left leg taking care to leave wood for the left ear, which is draped over the foot. Remove excess wood below the left leg and round the left side of belly. Round the legs and shape the feet.

Mark the tail and remove wood from the side of the left hip leaving the tail. Round the hip and the tail. Shape the right hip and hock.

Round the back up to the backbone. Using a gouge, cut along each side of the backbone, leaving it raised about 1/8 inch. Carve between and on each side of the shoulder blades, leaving them raised 1/8 inch as well. Carve excess from each side of the neck in back of the ears; then round the neck.

Carve away excess wood from each side of

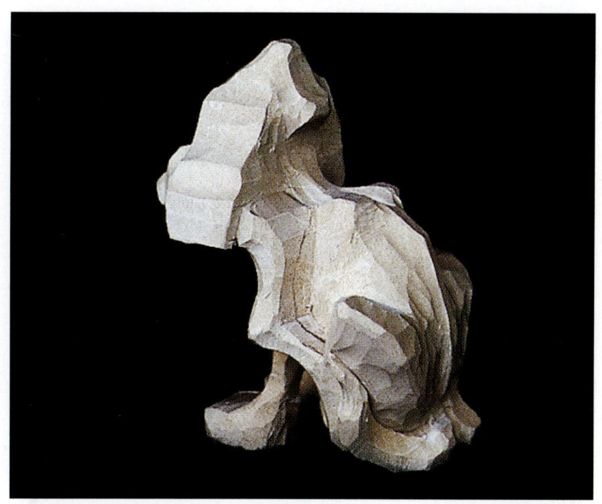

Angle view, roughed out

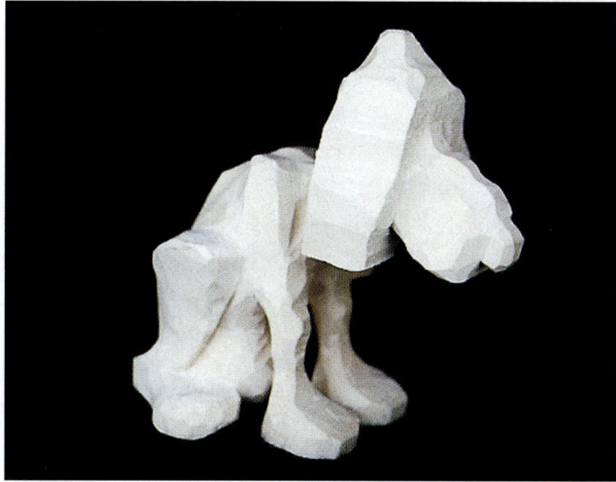

Angle view, roughed out

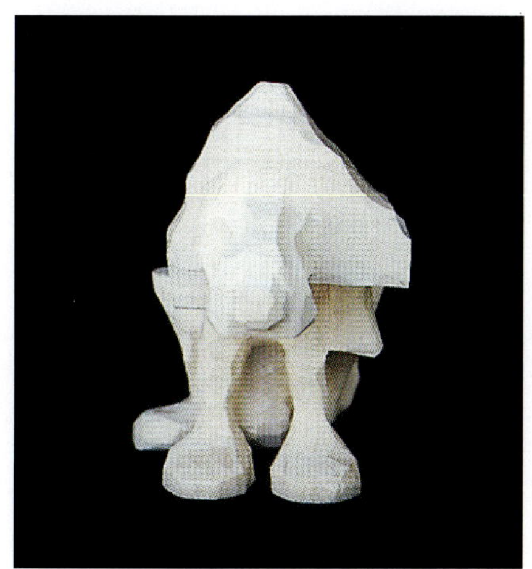

Front view, roughed out

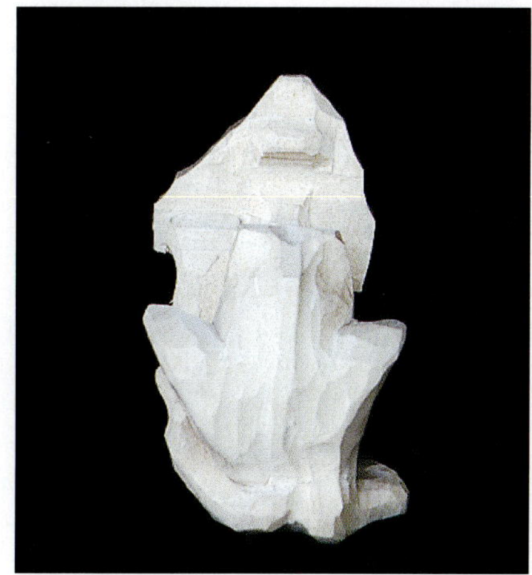

Back view, roughed out

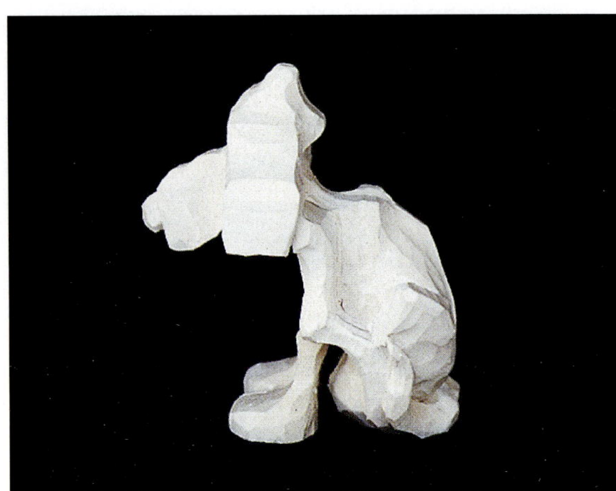

Side view, roughed out

the snout and the nose. Round the nose and the top of the snout.

DETAIL CARVING

Use small gouges to carve the separation between the left leg and the body and beneath the ear being scratched. Carve the separations between the hips and the body. Carve the toe separations and the toenails. Carve the ridges in Flea-bitis' backbone with a 2 mm veiner.

Shape the ears. The right ear will hang at an angle with the front portion touching the head. Use a gouge and a veiner to remove the wood from behind the right ear to the jaw. Carve the left ear so it bends forward and over part of the paw.

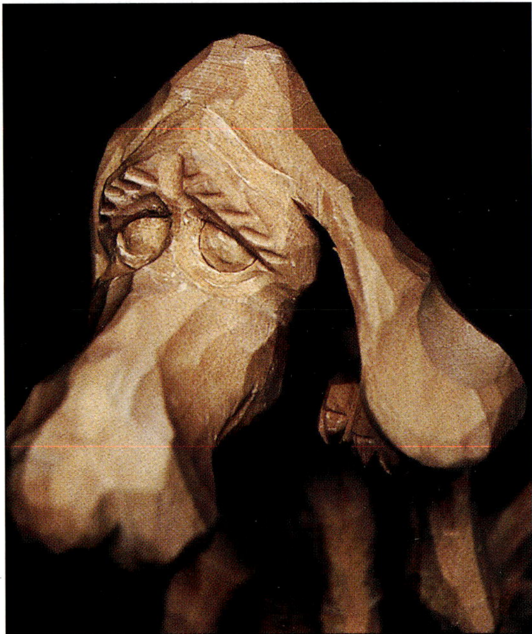

Close up of head and left foot, carving complete

Carve the mouth line. The upper lip will protrude slightly over the mouth. Shape the snout and carve the eyes as described in previous projects. Leave wood above the eyes for the drooping eye brows. Carve above each brow to make it stand out. Use a small veiner or a v-tool to carve the hair on the brows. Carve the wrinkles above the brows with a v-tool.

PAINTING AND FINISHING

Flea-bitis' body is burnt umber with black blended on the belly, the feet, the tips of the ears and the tail, the top of the head, the ridge of the snout and both sides of the nose. The nose and the brows are black. Paint the eyeballs white with black dots and the insides of the eyelids cadmium red light. Make "whiskers" with a sharp-tipped woodburner or the point of a pencil. Apply the antiquing.

MUTT McCOY

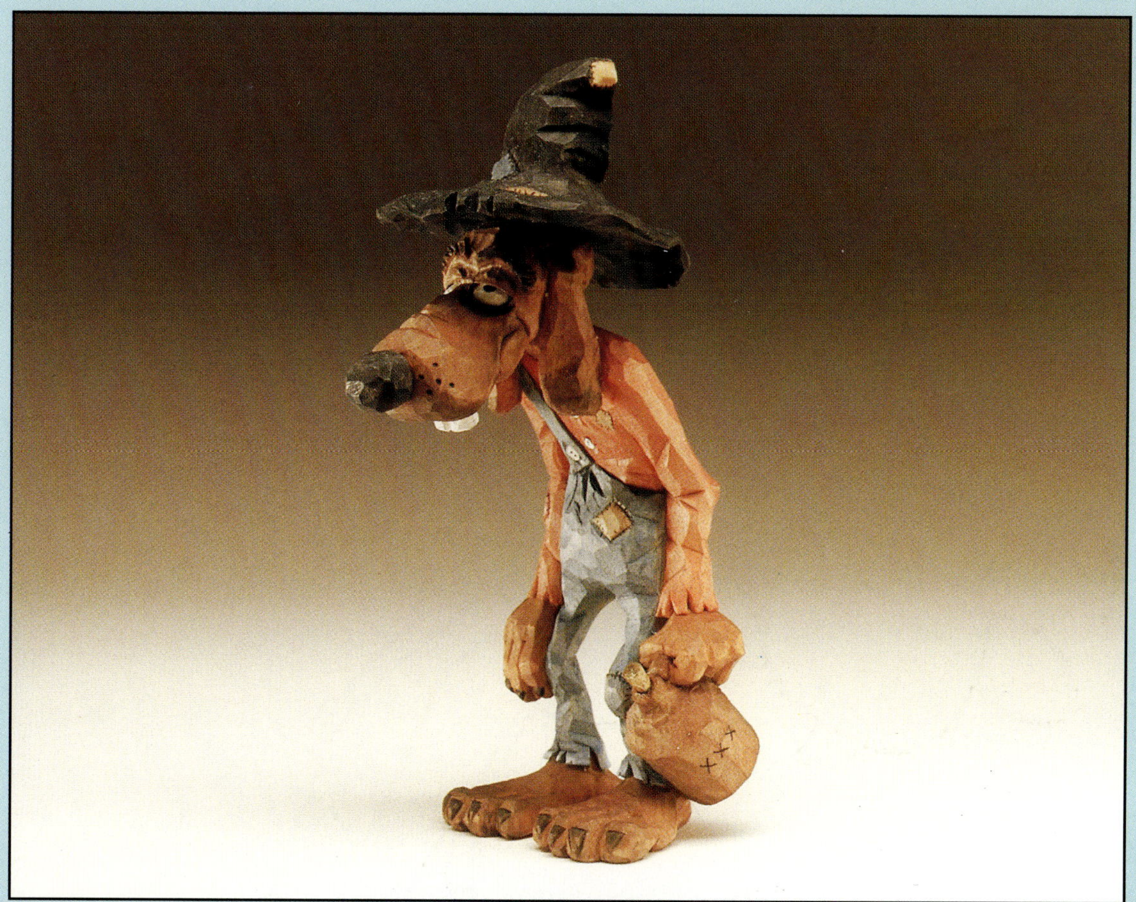

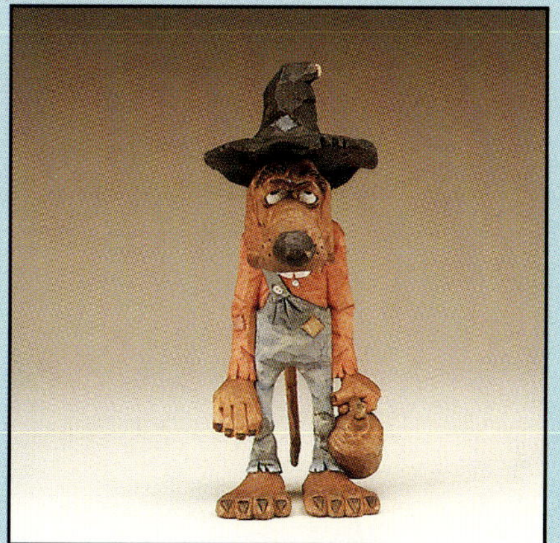

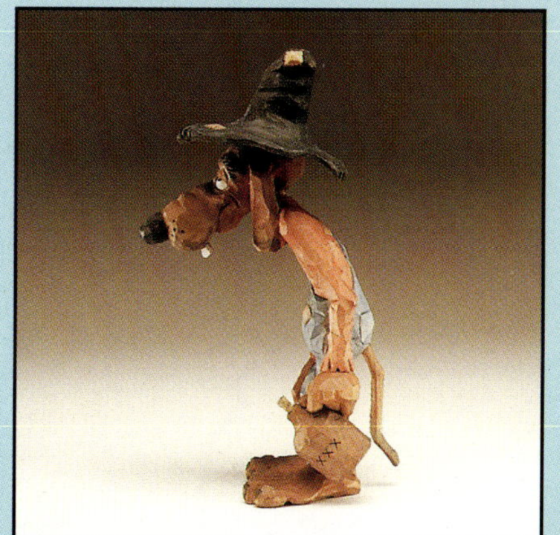

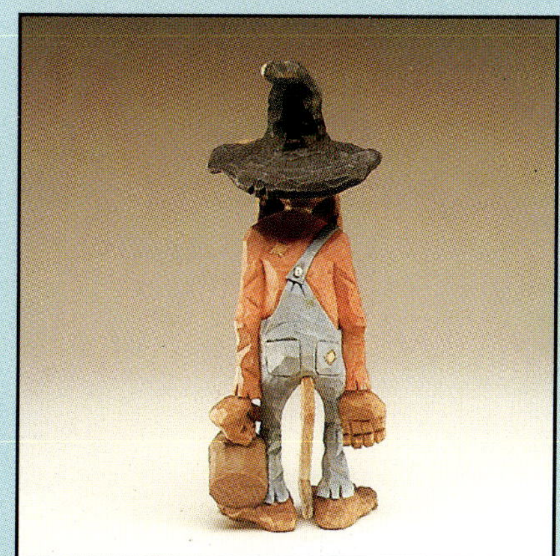

This old hound dog has been "humanized" somewhat by dressing him up as a hillbilly. Carving the left hand holding the whiskey jug is the most difficult.

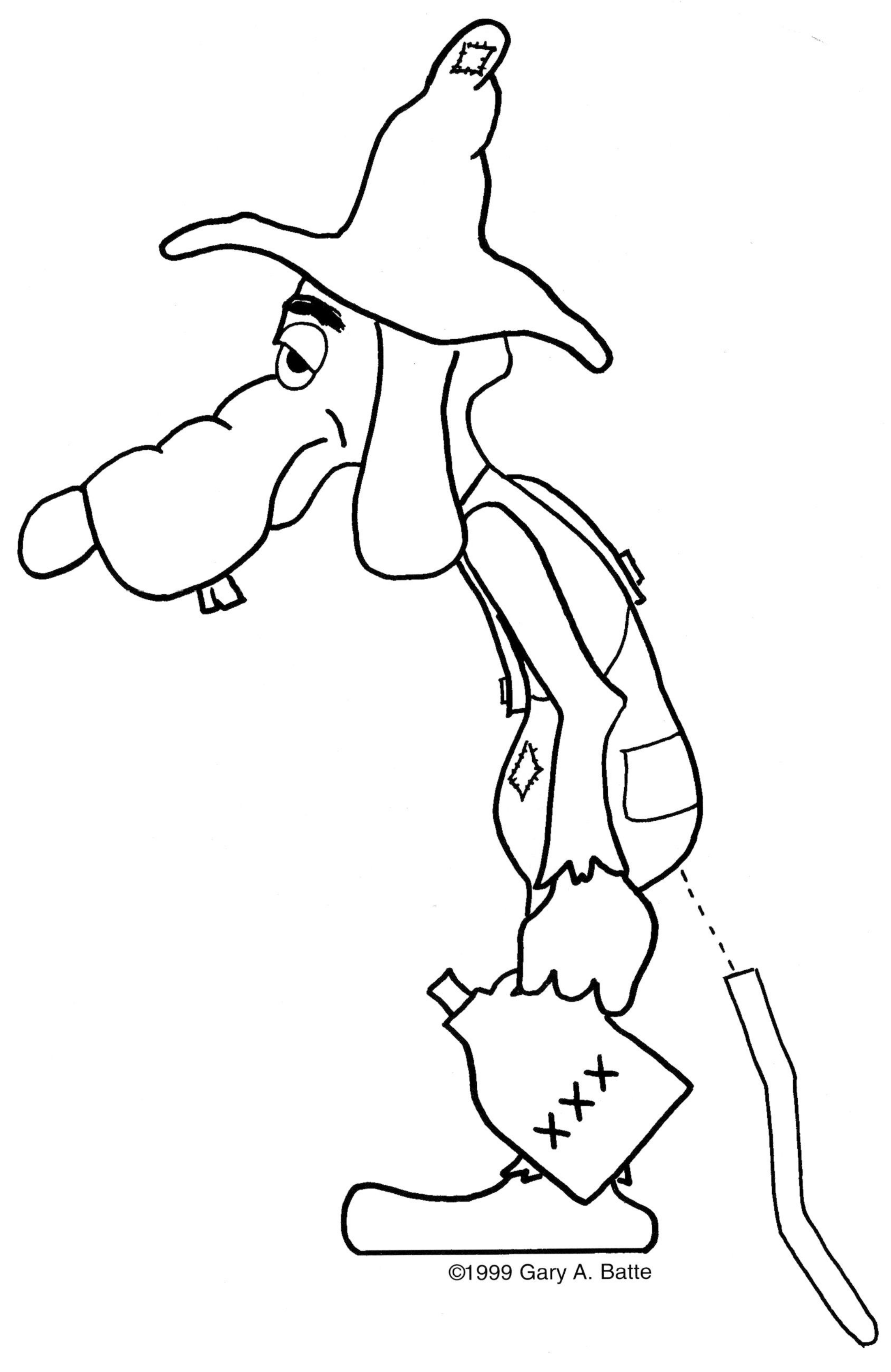

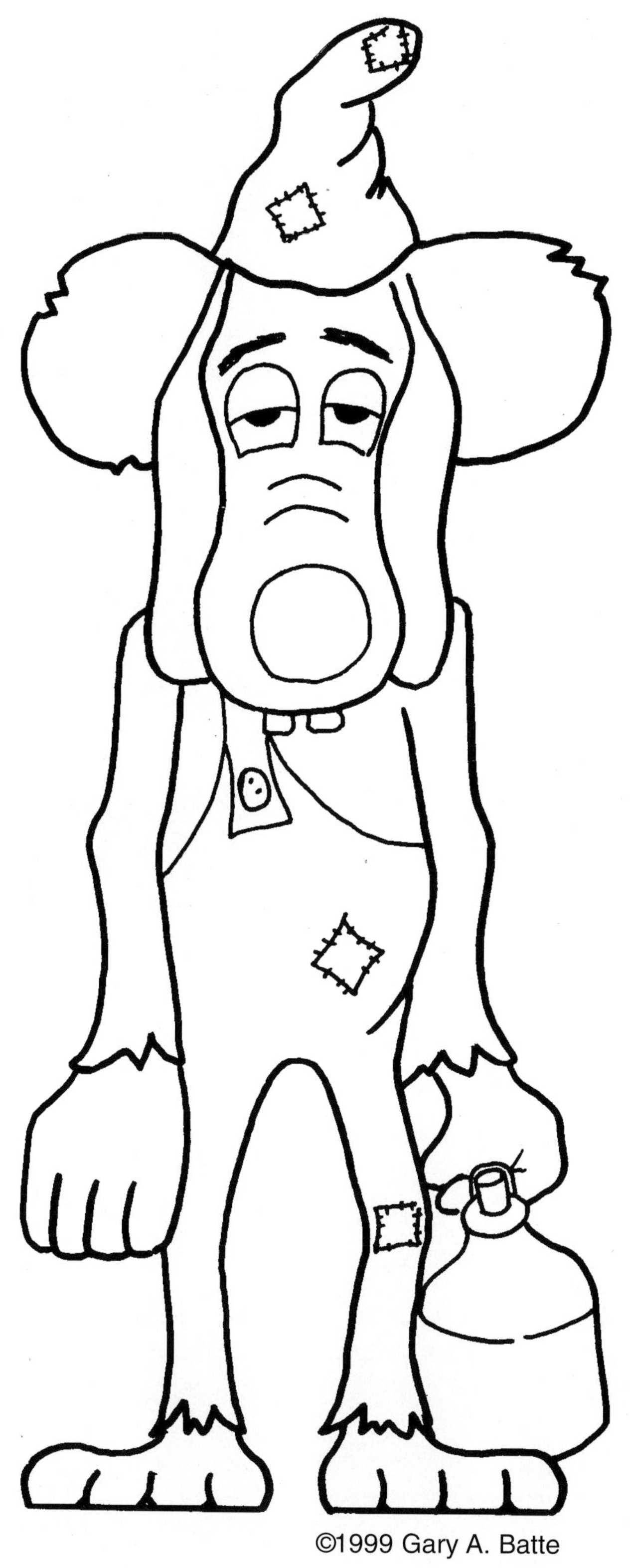

©1999 Gary A. Batte

I discovered Mutt McCoy wandering around in the Ozark hills near Dogpatch, Arkansas, when I was on vacation. At first glance, I thought I had found Harold Enlow, the famous woodcarver. Upon closer inspection, I saw a jug of white lightnin' in one hand and knew right away it wasn't him: Harold only drinks goat's milk. An even closer look revealed that what I was seeing was actually a hound dog dressed in some of Harold's old clothes. This inspired me to do a carving for this book.

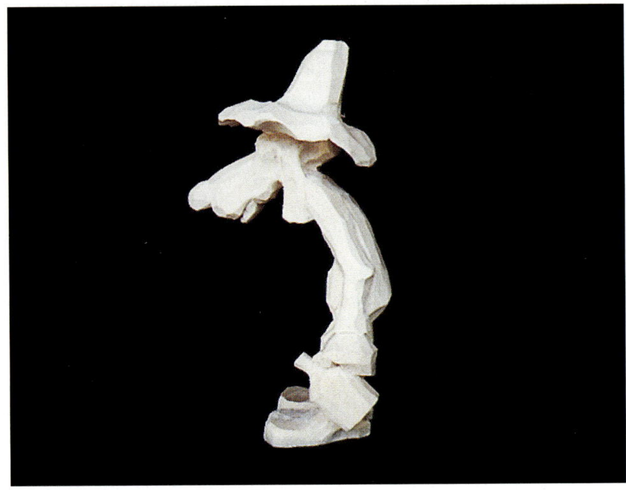
Side view, roughed out

ROUGHING OUT

Bandsaw the side view first; then the front view. You won't be able to saw out the front view of the hat because of the angle of the brim; just stop at the lowest point, which is the back edge of the brim.

Remove surplus wood from the hat and round the brim and the crown. The brim is floppy, so mark the wavy edges and then remove wood from both sides of the brim. It's a good idea to leave the brim a little thick until you near the end of the carving process to avoid breakage.

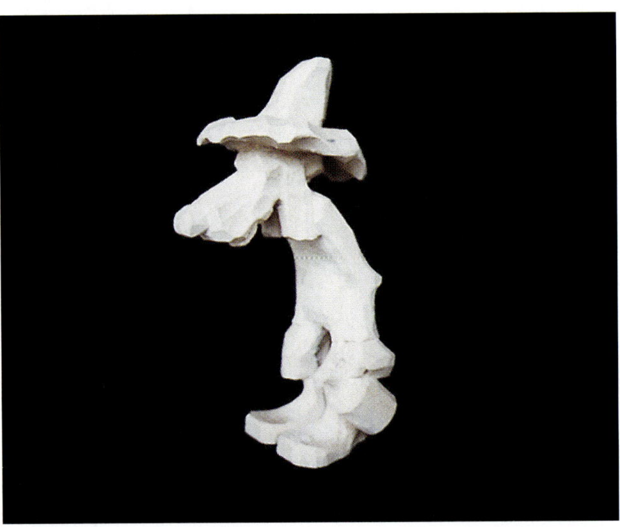
Angle view, roughed out

Remove some wood from in front of and in back of each ear. Carve excess wood from the side of the snout. Round the head, the neck, the nose and the top of the snout, leaving wood for the ears. Remove excess wood from in front of and in back of both arms and legs. Round the arms, legs and body, leaving extra wood for the elbows and knees to protrude. Refer to the pattern and mark the bottom of both feet. Shape the feet and the right front paw.

Carving the jug and the left paw is probably the toughest step in this carving. Square off the

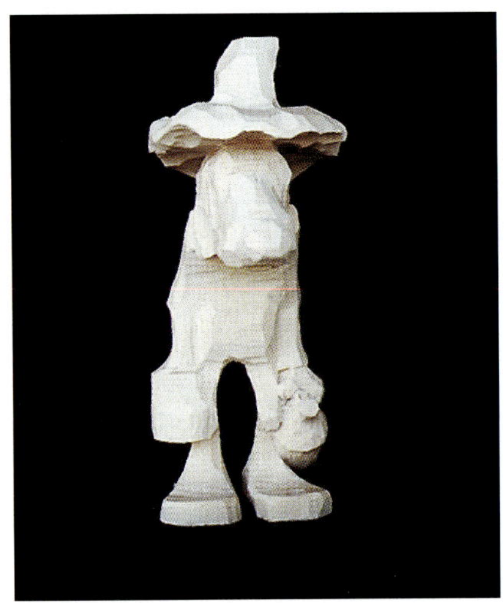
Front view, roughed out

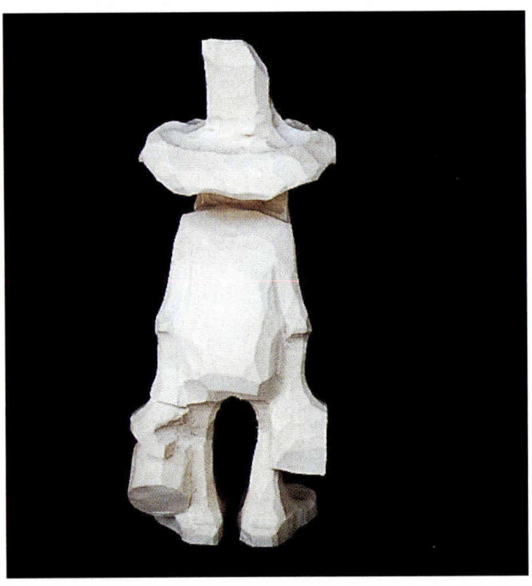
Back view, roughed out

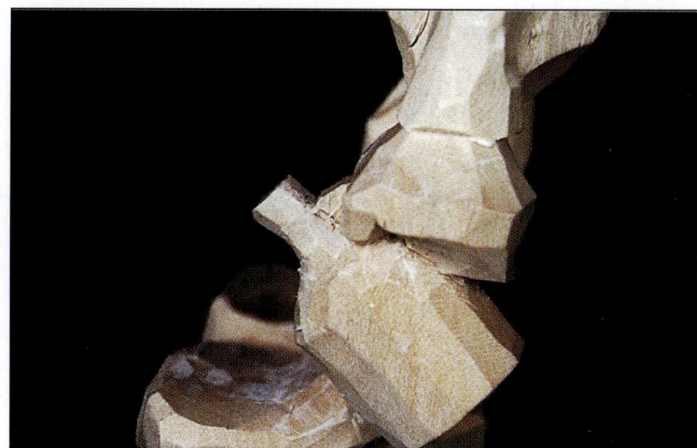

Paw holding jug, roughed out

sides and the bottom of the jug; then draw a centerline. Mark the toes, one passing through the jug's handle. Carve the neck of the jug first, leaving wood for the handle and the toes. Carve the side view of the handle, leaving the toe that passes through it. Mark the top view of the handle and remove the excess wood from both sides. Round the rest of the jug and finish the paw to fit the jug.

DETAIL CARVING

Make knife cuts near the top portion of the crown to create a bend to one side. Remove a wedge of wood from behind each ear. Outline the area with knife cuts; then remove wood with a gouge. Continue carving alongside the neck until there is an open space between the neck and the ear. Finish carving the ear and rounding the neck.

Shape the ears with a knife. Refer to the Sweet Pea project for carving the eyes. Remove some wood above each eyebrow with a gouge and carve hair on the eyebrows with a v-tool or a small veiner. Carve the two front teeth and the mouth. Carve two grooves across the top of the nose with a v-tool or a knife.

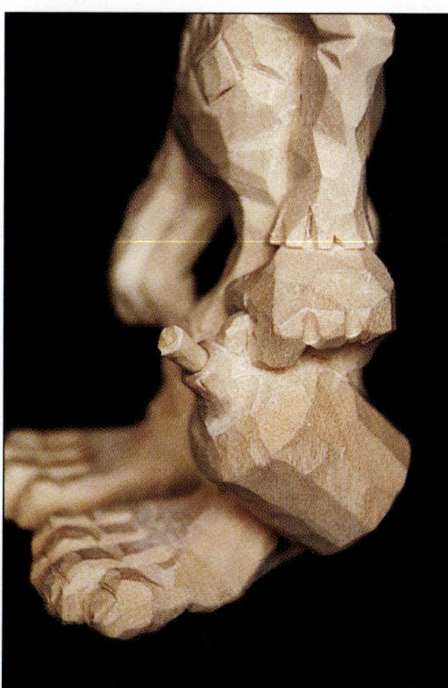

Paw holding jug, carving complete

Carve separations between the legs and the body and round them, leaving the elbows and knees protruding.

Carve toe separations and toenails.

Remove some wood below the trouser cuffs. To create a ragged edge, remove v-shaped pieces of wood from the cuff line.

Carve the trousers strap by making stop cuts along the edges with a knife tip; then remove a small amount of wood next to the strap. Use the same technique to carve separations between the pants and the shirt. Carve several wrinkles adjacent to each end of the strap with a v-tool. The strap buttons are carved by pressing a 3 mm veiner into the wood at the upper and lower edges of the button; then use the veiner to scoop a little wood from above the top cut and from below the bottom cut. Use a wood burner tip or a sharp pencil to make button holes. Carve the shirt buttons in a similar manner using a #6 – 3 mm straight gouge. The pockets, patches and wrinkles in the shirt and the pants are carved with a knife. Create the stitches on the patches with a woodburner or a sharp pencil.

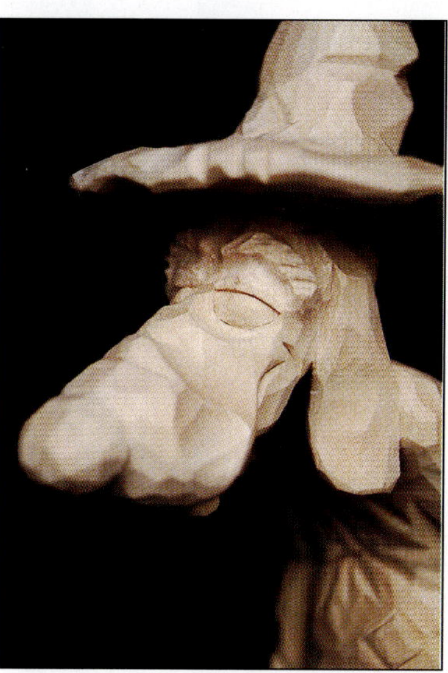

Head, carving complete

The tail is carved separately. Drill a 3/16-inch hole at the point of attachment. Wait to attach the tail until the piece has been painted and antiqued.

PAINTING AND FINISHING

Mutt's head, ears, paws and feet are painted with burnt sienna mixed with raw umber. Black is blended along the top of the snout and on the tips of the ears and the tail. The toenails, the brows, the nose and the hat are all black. Paint the pants denim with white buttons and add patches of various colors. Use napthol red light mixed with a small amount of raw umber to paint the shirt. Mutt's teeth are white. The eyeballs are white with black half-dots painted just underneath the eye lids. Paint the jug with a mixture of sweetheart blush and raw umber. After the carving is antiqued and dry, glue the tail in place.

Books by the Experts

JOHN NELSON SCROLL SAW

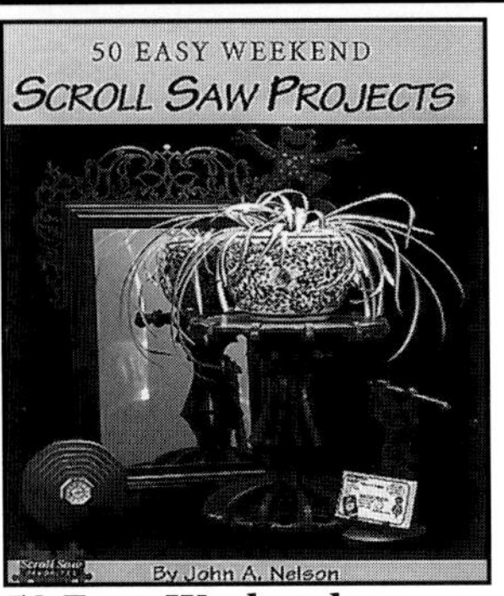

50 Easy Weekend Scroll Saw Projects
1-56523-108-2
$9.95
By John Nelson
50 patterns for beautiful and practical projects. Ready to use patterns.

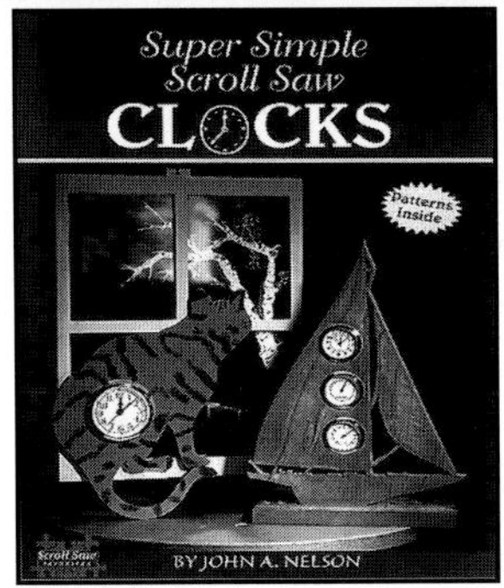

Super Simple Clocks Scroll Saw
1-56523-111-2
$9.95
By John Nelson
With your scroll saw and quartz clock movements you can easily make these 50 examples.

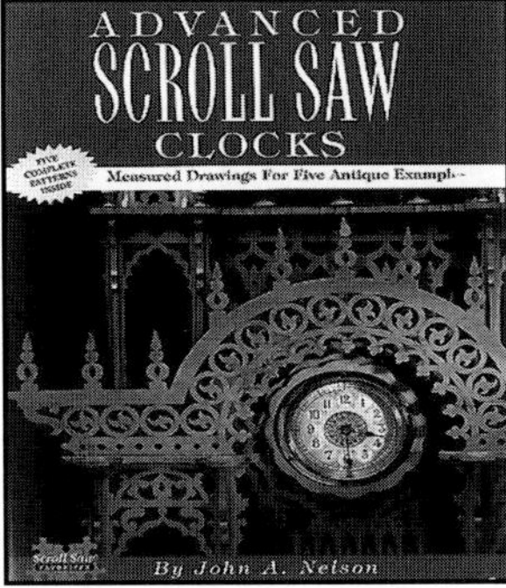

Advanced Scroll Saw Clocks
1-56523-110-4
$9.95
By John Nelson
Five amazing projects never before published. Complete, ready to use patterns.

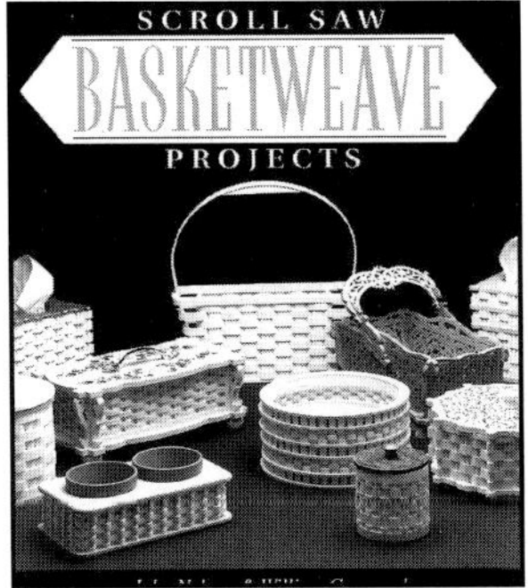

Scroll Saw Basketweave Projects
1-56523-103-1
$9.95
By John Nelson/William Guimond
12 all-new projects for making authentic looking baskets on your scroll saw.

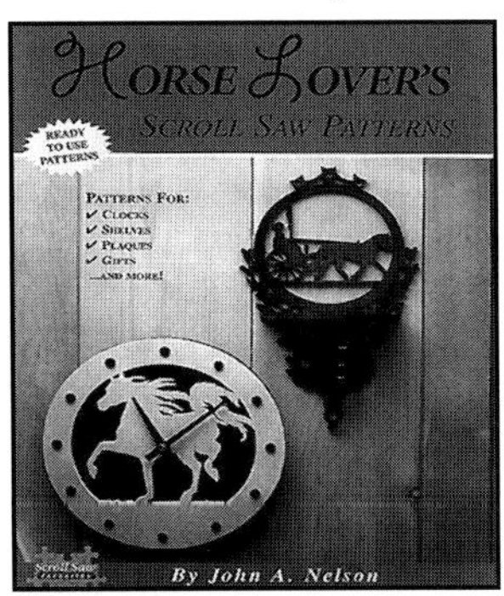

Horse Lovers Scroll Saw Projects
1-56523-109-0
$9.95
By John Nelson
A terrific collection of all-new projects from this popular author. Ready to use patterns.

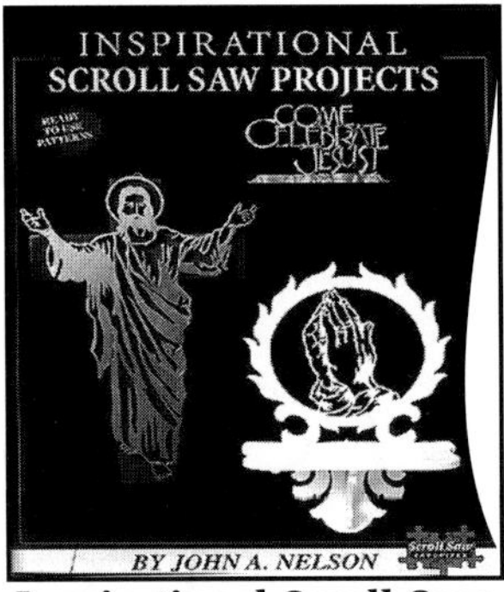

Inspirational Scroll Saw Projects
1-56523-112-0
$9.95
By John Nelson
50 plus projects to beautifully reflect your faith.

WOODCARVING BOOKS

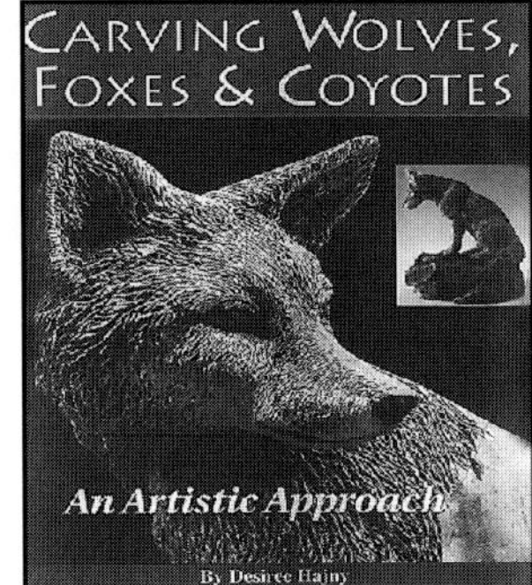

Carving Wolves, Foxes & Coyotes: *An Artistic Approach*
1-56523-098-1
$19.95
By Desiree Hajny
The most complete canine guide in color. Techniques, reference photos, anatomy charts, and patterns for foxes, wolves and coyotes.

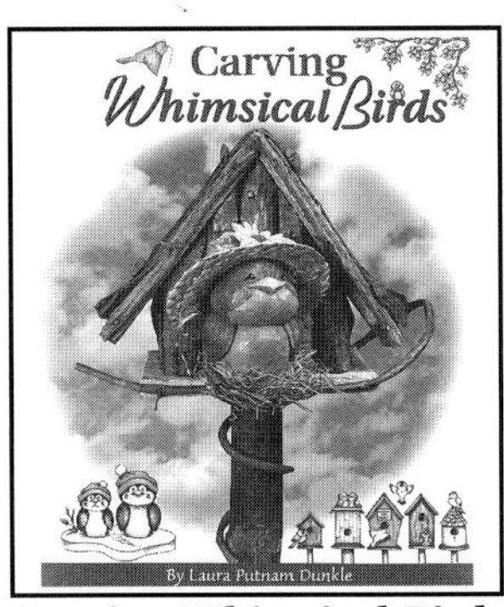

Carving Whimsical Birds
1-56523-113-9
$12.95
By Laura Putnam Dunkle
Easy, fun and quick to carve! Good book for the beginner–uses commercial turnings.

Folk and Figure Carving
1-56523-105-8
$14.95
By Ross Oar
Explore caricature and realistic carvings in the 15 projects inside.

MISCELLANEOUS BOOKS

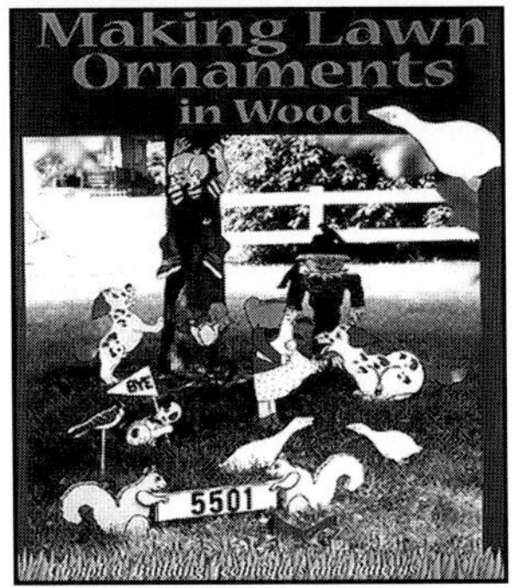

Making Lawn Ornaments in Wood ~ 2nd Edition
1-56523-104-X
$14.95
By Paul Meisel
New edition with 16 pages of new patterns. Only book on the subject. Includes 20 ready to use full-size patterns. Strong seller.

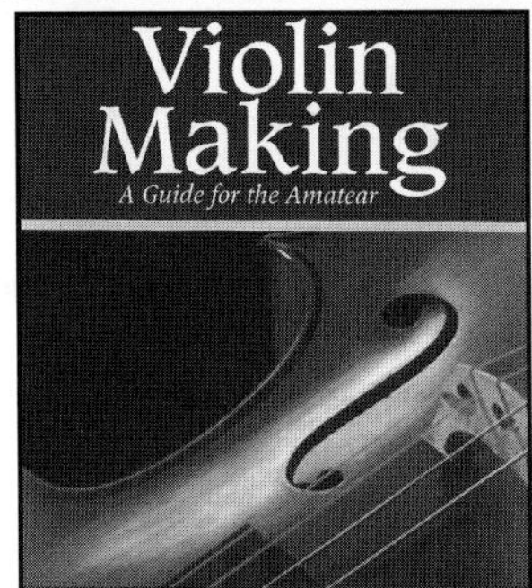

Violin Making A Guide for the Amateur
1-56523-091-4
$14.95
By Bruce Ossman
The easiest book on making violins in the home workshop. Complete set of plans included.

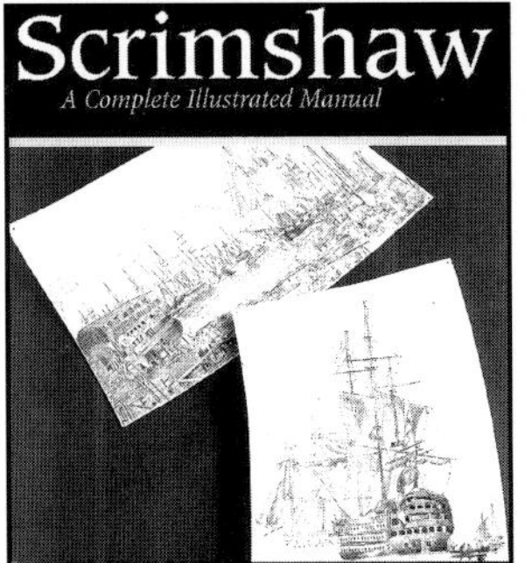

Scrimshaw: A Complete Illustrated Manual
1-56523-095-7
$14.95
By Roger Schroeder & Steve Paszkiewicz
Gorgeous full color guide for the artist and craftsperson. Step-by-step techniques and patterns.

Try your local book dealer first!

Canada and Foreign orders please pay in US funds using a cashier's check or by credit card (include expiration date). Please list daytime phone number for processing questions.

Shipping & handling: $2.50 per book • $5.00 maximum over 2 books

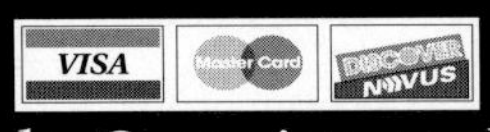

E-mail: sales@carvingworld.com

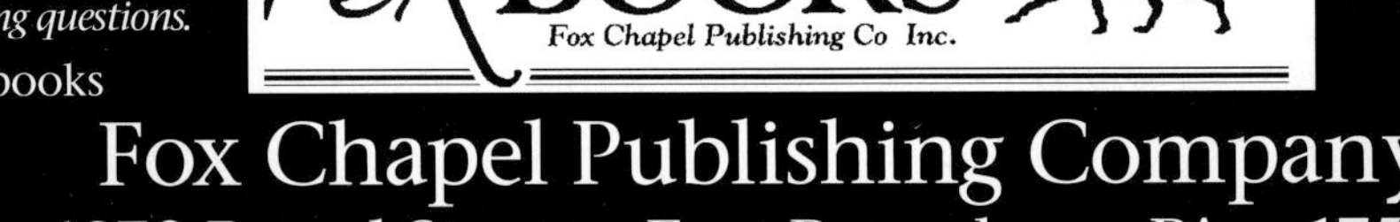

Fox Chapel Publishing Company
1970 Broad Street • East Petersburg, PA • 1752

More Books by the Experts

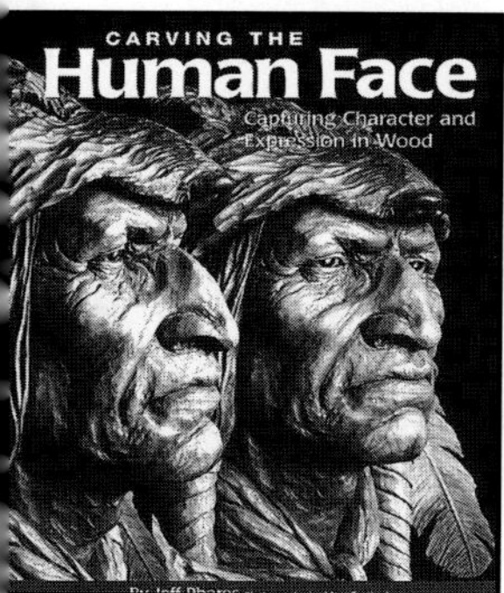

Carving the Human Face
By Jeff Phares
The best book available on carving faces! A full color guide is included.
104 pages, 8.5x11", soft cover.
$24.95 • 1-56523-102-3

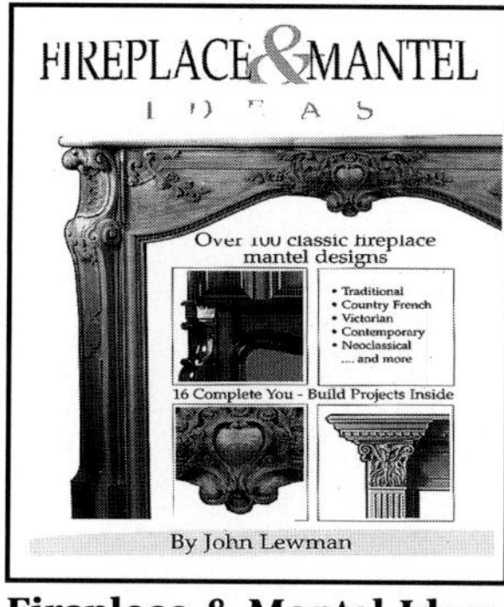

Fireplace & Mantel Ideas
By John Lewman
15 ready-to-use patterns and hundreds of photos showing installation and design.
90 pages, 8.5x11, soft cover.
$19.95 • 1-56523-106-6

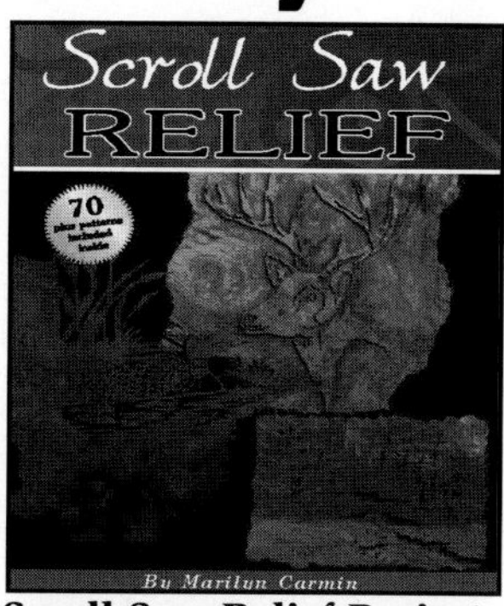

Scroll Saw Relief Projects
By Marilyn Carmin
The first book on fret and relief work. Includes more than 100 patterns.
120 pages, 8.5x11, soft cover.
$14.95 • 1-56523-107-4

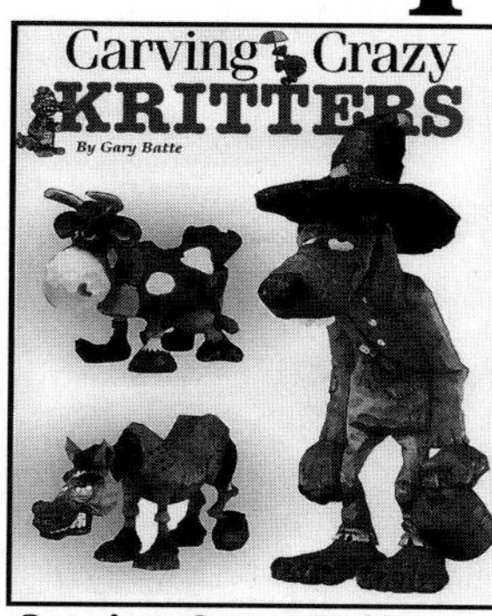

Carving Crazy Kritters
By Gary Batte
Full of creative new designs for caricature animals. A real winner!
64 pages, 8.5x11, soft cover.
$14.95 • 1-56523-114-7

Creative Christmas Carvings
By Tina Toney
A beautiful and practical full-color guide to exciting holiday carving projects.
64 pages, 8.5x11, soft cover.
$14.95 • 1-56523-120-1

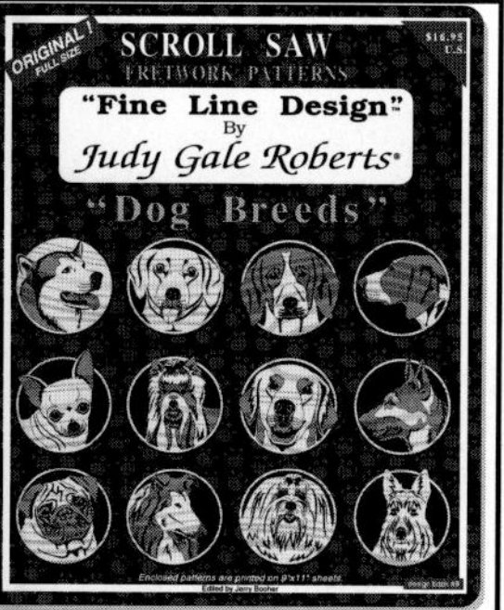

Scroll Saw Fretwork Patterns ~ Dog Breeds
By Judy Gale Roberts
Includes dozens of all-new designs of "man's best friend".
60 pages, 8.5x11, soft cover-spiral bound.
$16.95 • 1-883083-08-7

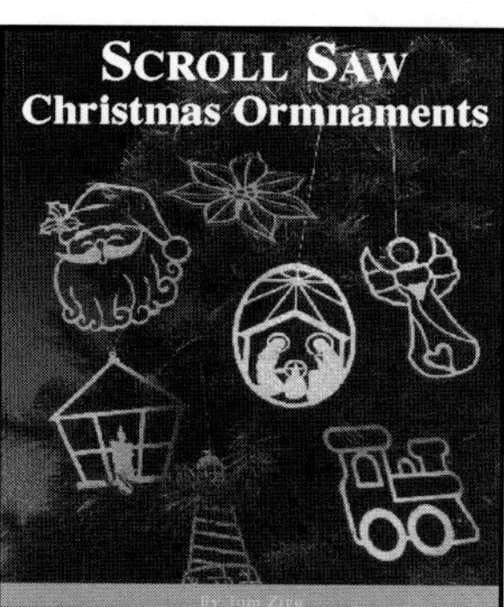

Scroll Saw Christmas Ornaments
By Tom Zieg
Over 200 ornament patterns, with brass, copper and plastic designs.
64 pages, 8.5x11, soft cover.
$9.95 • 1-56523-123-6

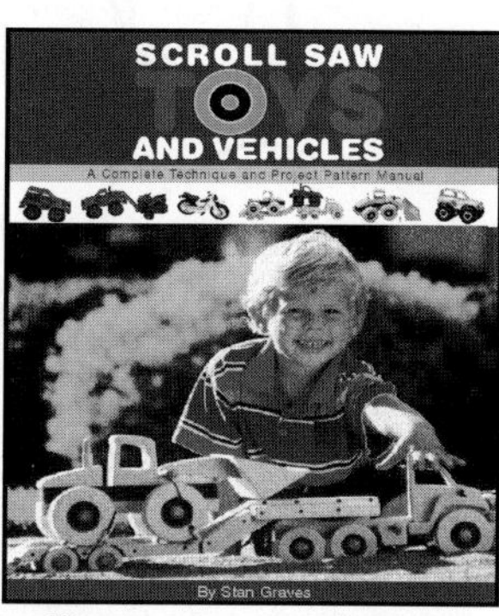

Scroll Saw Toys and Vehicles Technique & Pattern Manual
By Stan Graves
Create easy, fun toys on your scroll saw with everyday materials.
56 pages, 8.5x11, soft cover.
$12.95 • 1-56523-115-5

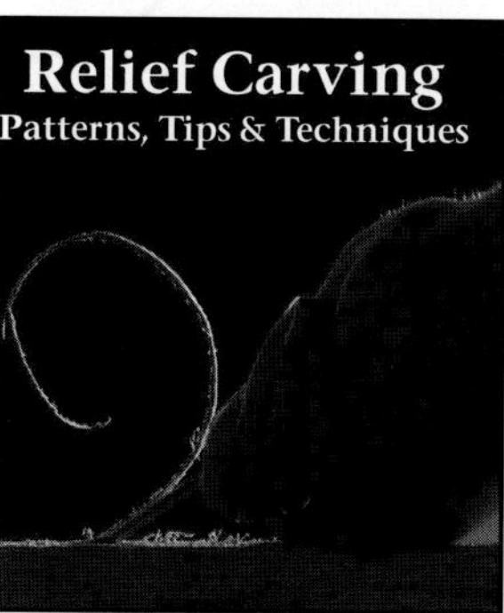

Relief Carving ~ Patterns, Tips & Techniques
By William F. Judt
A complete introduction to relief carving. Learn tricks of the trade!
120 pages, 8.5x11, soft cover.
$19.95 • 1-56523-124-4

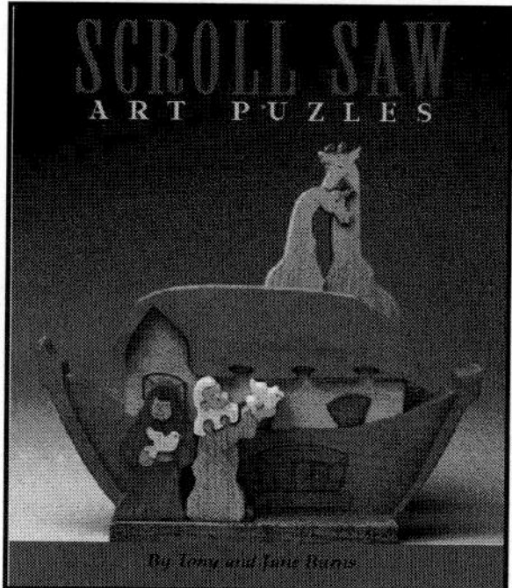

Scroll Saw Art Puzzles
By Tony and June Burns
Includes 32 patterns for cute, classical and whimsical puzzles.
80 pages, 8.5x11, soft cover.
$14.95 • 1-56523-116-3

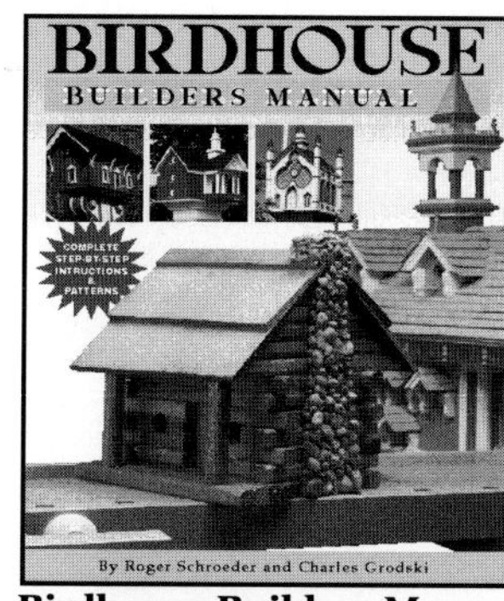

Birdhouse Builders Manual
By Roger Schroeder and Charles Grodshi
Full patterns, step-by-step photos and instructions. Sure to please!
120 pages, 8.5x11, soft cover.
$19.95 • 1-56523-100-7

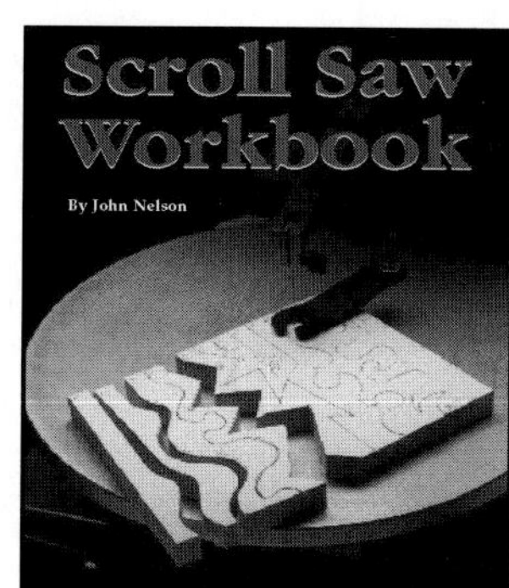

Scroll Saw Workbook
By John Nelson
The best beginner's technique book from noted author John Nelson.
96 pages, 8.5x11, soft cover.
$14.95 • 1-56523-117-1

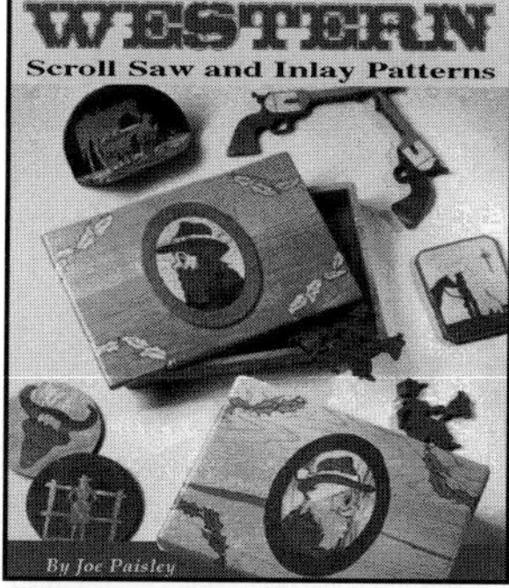

Western Scroll Saw and Inlay Patterns
By Joe Paisley
Exciting new inlay techniques and lots of new western patterns.
100 pages, 8.5x11, soft cover.
$14.95 • 1-56523-118-X

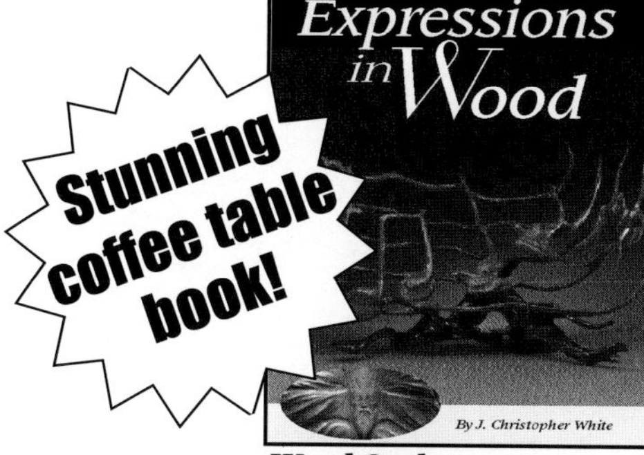

Wood Sculptures ~ Expressions In Wood
By J. Christopher White
Stylized carved wooden sculpture at its best.
128 pages, 9x12, hard cover.
$34.95 • 1-56523-122-8

Try your local book dealer first!

Canada and Foreign orders please pay in US funds using a cashier's check or credit card (include expiration date). Please list daytime phone number for processing questions.

Shipping & handling: $2.50 per book • $5.00 maximum over 2 books

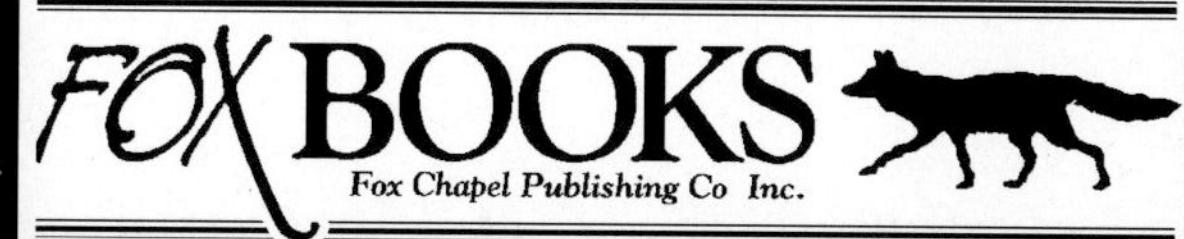

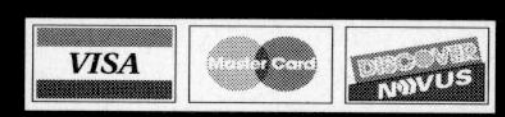

Fox Chapel Publishing Company
E-mail: sales@carvingworld.com
1970 Broad Street • East Petersburg, PA • 17520